CAN'T STEAL MY JOY

THE JOURNEY TO A
DIFFERENT KIND OF BRAVE

BEKAH BOWMAN

WWW.CANTSTEALMYJOY.COM

www.cantstealmyjoy.com

Edited by Anne Riley. Flower design by Anna Bloomfield. Cover design by Jessica Salas. Interior design by Typewriter Creative Co. Author photo by Debbie Gardner.

ISBN 978-1-7331519-0-0 (Paperback)
ISBN 978-1-7331519-1-7 (eBook)

It seems obvious I would dedicate this book to the 3 boys in my life: Danny (my hubby), Titus and Ely. And I absolutely do. This journey has never been just mine. These three other individuals have journeyed it too, and we have and will continue to do this life together.

I can't move along, though, before I also dedicate this to our incredible Team 4 Titus & Ely tribe. I sit here trying to find adequate words to even express the ways in which you all have carried us. This story is written the way it is because you were the hands and feet of Jesus. You showed up with generous open arms and gathered our broken souls in, lifting us to the One who could redeem.

To Danny, Titus, Ely and our incredible tribe—This one's for you.

TABLE OF CONTENTS

PROLOGUE

've had this profound revelation sinking its teeth into my mind. It's changing me. I almost feel like writing about this first is giving you the end of the book before you've had a chance to fall in love with the characters. But that's when God reminds me there is more. There's more to this story, His story. And while what I'm learning now feels like a culmination, it's not. It's all part of the journey. And it's one I continue to learn and re-learn.

In this particular journey of mine, I thought I knew the best way for God to show up. I expected things to just work out. I figured I would be capable and skilled at solving the problems that might saunter across my life's journey. But God began teaching me that I was actually quite blind.

I began to learn that the biggest way He could show up in my life was through a great healing. Not the kind I wanted, but the kind I desperately needed. So, I began to pray for that. A healing of my heart, of the hearts of those we shared life with, and of your heart as well.

It came at a cost.

And I was asked to live in our hard moments intentionally.

I was called to be vulnerable and real about the despair and sadness I felt while not allowing it to swallow me whole and paralyze me.

But looking back, I can't think of a better way for God to redeem what we have been through than to heal our hearts. So, it was worth the risk to open up, to take the next right step on days that felt way too hard, and to spread a message of hope that I was experiencing deep in my bones.

Herein is where *Can't Steal My Joy* was born. It's all about the heart change, my friend. Welcome to the journey to a different kind of brave.

Thanks for listening,

Bekah

PART ONE

A DARK UNKNOWN

CHAPTER ONE

LOSING CONTROL

It was a Monday. February 10, 2014, to be exact. I had dropped Titus, my three-year-old son, off at preschool for the morning. My mom was visiting from out of town and we were out with my seven-month-old son, Ely, shopping. My phone had sunk down into the diaper bag. (Can I just call it the Mary Poppins bag? It held alllll the things.) Not only had my phone sunk down to the bottom, but I had accidentally left it on silent. As I was trying on a cute pair of boots, my mom's phone rang. She looked at the caller ID, "Oh, it's Danny."

My husband. *Whoops*, I thought. As she answered, I started searching through the bag to find my phone. He had likely tried calling me already. (This happens often.) I overheard, "Sure, hang on..." My mom handed me her phone.

"Hey!" I said, beginning to explain why I didn't answer my phone. But I didn't get a chance as his urgent voice spoke over mine. I glanced at my phone. TWELVE missed calls?

"Titus had a seizure. 911 was called..." Danny was still talking but my brain was whirling. He had a WHAT? A seizure? How? Why?

"Titus. Seizure!" I squeaked to my mom in the middle of the shoe department. My feet started running to the car before my mind could even process what was happening. I heard Danny say, "I'm on my way. I'm almost there." We hung up as I reached the car in the parking lot. I jumped in, started up the ignition, and realized I just left my mom and Ely in the dust. I gathered half my mind back, jumped out and grabbed Ely, car seat and all from my mom who came rushing after me. After I loaded Ely up, we climbed in the car and began the trek across town to my oldest son. *Oh, my son.... A seizure!* My inner narrative began constructing all the possible scenarios that could have caused a seizure. I wondered what I would find when I got there.

"Take a deep breath, Bekah," I heard my mom chime in. "We'll get there, but we need to get there safely."

I looked at the speedometer. *Right. Come on, Bek. Slow down. Danny is probably there now with him.* I breathed. But scared tears burned in the backs of my eyes; something wasn't right.

I got to the front desk. Urgently, I told them my son had been brought in by ambulance. They ushered me back quickly. Without a word to my mom, I followed. I knew she would take care of Ely. Titus needed me. I bee-lined it for his room, not able to get there fast enough. I rounded the corner and to my relief, I saw my husband had already made it there. He had gathered his mini-me, our Titus, in his arms. I could see it in his eyes—the protector was present and ready to do anything in his power to shield his son from whatever this was. I jumped in the bed with them waiting for the doctor.

Martha, my co-worker and our church secretary, had arrived in the waiting room, per a text from my mom. She was our emergency contact on our school form for Titus. I always thought those were so silly. Of course, I would answer the phone if the school ever called. But on this day, when our son was rushed to the hospital by ambulance, Danny was in a meeting and hadn't answered the call that was from a number he didn't recognize. I, as you know, had mine buried and on silent. Martha had received the third call from the school and proceeded to try to contact me (again, buried, silent phone) and then Danny, who finally answered. Martha had climbed in her car immediately after talking with Danny to come support us in whatever way we needed. I tried not to beat myself up over missing twelve, count 'em—twelve missed calls at a time my son needed me. I turned my attention to him next to me.

Titus was lethargic from the unexpected seizure. His face pale and countenance foggy; he was aware enough to know we were there. He wanted his mommy and daddy. I wanted answers. Answers and solutions to fix this so it never happened again.

The doctor came in and suggested a CAT scan to see if an injury may have caused the seizure. They asked if he'd been sick lately. No. He hadn't. They took his temperature and checked for infections. His temperature was fine. Everything came back negative.

"Some kids have a seizure," the doctor stated, "and then never have another one. This seizure could've been caused by an infection we can't see yet. Otherwise, he looks totally fine. We are going to discharge you and encourage you to follow up with a neurologist."

And with that, we were sent home with a load full of mystery, a small pamphlet on seizure protocol, and a non-urgent referral to a neurologist.

We went home and collapsed with emotional exhaustion. A favorite movie went on. Someone dropped off dinner for the evening. And we waited. For what, we weren't sure, but it was the beginning of something eerie that had just invaded our home.

At 6:00 the next morning, I heard an otherworldly cry come from Titus's room. I bolted out of our bed and ran the hallway between us, bursting through his door to his bedside. He laid there in his bed, his arms curled in toward his chest, his head pulled by an unseen force to the top right corner of the room, his eyes fixed in that direction. His whole body shook and his lips were turning blue. *Oh God! God, he's seizing again. Stop it, please!* I cried in desperate whispers. Danny rounded the corner and together we pleaded with Titus to come back.

"It's okay, Titus. Mommy and Daddy are here," I said to him. "I love you, buddy. You are so strong. It's okay, come back to us sweetie, come back to us." Minutes later, the seizure faded and left him pale and drained again. We gathered his long frame into our arms and held him, tears flowing.

The notion this was a onetime happenstance flew out the window.

I was on the phone as soon as the neurology office opened. April. They could see him in April. I tried to explain the urgency of our case, but hung up the phone defeated. How would we last two months?

My next call was to our pediatrician for an appointment to be seen that day. Before we got in to see her, Titus had a third seizure. She made a call herself to the neurologist and scheduled an appointment for the following week. It wasn't until we were back in her office again the following day with more seizures to report that we were given the option to take someone else's cancellation for February 14. So it was on Valentine's Day, four days after Titus's first seizure that we headed up to the University of Chicago to find help. The neurologist put him on anti-epileptic medication and sent us home, a diagnosis of epilepsy in our hands. Our son was suddenly and mysteriously experiencing a cruel and debilitating symptom of something we couldn't put our finger on. Medication and a name seemed to help us feel we were doing something. Little did we know, this relief would be short-lived.

My younger son, Ely, began having his own health issues around the same time. As if all that was thrown at us with Titus wasn't enough, Ely was slated for a major surgery to repair his stomach and put in a feeding tube. For several months, he had been unable to keep anything down. At ten months of age he was labeled "failure to thrive."

I remember walking to my boss' office around that time. I rarely fell apart in front of others, but tears of fear came to the surface as I updated him on our family. He did what a good pastor would do. He prayed with me. When we were done, he looked at me, gave a little grin and said, "Have you ever heard the story of the ten plagues?"

He always had a way with words. I sarcastically chuckled and thanked him for the support and encouragement. His statement, though delivered comedic relief, rang true in my heart. Were we ever going to catch a break?

In the months that followed, we moved from Chicago out to Irvine, California for my husband's job. As we navigated new surroundings, new doctors and life without an established support system, our routine was stripped of predictability. Our son began to drop, shake and seize out of nowhere. At home. At night. At the grocery store. At the kids' discovery center. At church. Anywhere and everywhere, this evil mystery monster stripped us of any control to protect our son. We were frantic. I felt as though I was fighting a giant who had ten arms, all swinging at once, and I had to fight back blindfolded. There was no way to anticipate when we'd take another hit, where to strike back, or how to shield him. There was no control.

We had no control.

We like control. We like a properly laid plan that executes well, brings us success, propels us forward. As Danny and I said our marriage vows to each other, made job choices and cross-country moves, decided the proper time to have kids, and bought a house, we held a perceived control through it all. We dictated when and what and how. And with a fair amount of accuracy, I might add!

My husband is a planner. He got a master's degree in organizational leadership, for goodness sake! He knows how to establish and follow a well-laid plan. I appreciate his strength in this area and feel great security in it, but I am a lover of spontaneity. I love a last-minute adventure. I love unexpected goodness popping out of nowhere. But this? Well, this was not on my terms. And it definitely wasn't good.

I put on my brave face each and every day to help Titus's school teachers, church teachers, friends, and family support him the best they could.

I put on my brave face every day to lead a family ministry at our church demonstrating that even in this, I wouldn't be deterred from serving Jesus.

I put on my brave face every day in every doctor's appointment as they tested and poked and prodded my son.

I put on my brave face with each medication I had to learn the name of and the tricks I learned to get Titus to swallow it.

I put on my brave face when Titus seized and I watched the clock tick, minutes that felt like eternity passing by.

But when I climbed in that shower with no one to watch, my brave face melted down the drain with the water and soap and I was a puddle of grief over my inability to gain control over this mess. I was helpless and falling into hopelessness.

This was the tension I lived in. I was attempting to faithfully follow what I thought God was asking of me, where He put me, and what had been laid in our laps to hold. And in that following, find a way to reconcile our circumstances with my understanding of God and His character. Surely, this was a great test of faith. And surely it would pass.

That was how I plunged into the following year. I Googled the heck out of seizures and other symptoms that began to show up in my son. Tremors, eye rolling, stumbling and falling, impulsivity and extreme anger, speech delay. I diagnosed him several times myself. We tried taking him to the chiropractor, getting massaged, using essential oils. We took him to special doctors who thought outside the box, did special testing, went to speech therapy, occupational therapy, and physical therapy.

It was safe to say we had gone several boxing rounds with this ten-armed monster and we were not done. There *had* to be something we could do to help our son. The option of no answers was just not acceptable to me, nor did I ever entertain the idea that I might not be able to regain control over this situation.

As Danny settled in to the new culture at work, his boss became a good friend. Danny rarely shared much about his workday with me, but one night, he shared that he had gone to his boss's office to talk. All that was going on with Titus was overwhelming. And for my husband, a man who wants to care for and protect his family, this was way out of whack. He shared a portion of their conversation with me.

"What if I can't do anything to help my son and he dies?" my husband had bravely verbalized.

His boss responded, "I guess I look at it this way. God has gifted my kids to me. They aren't mine. They are His. As long as I have them here with me, I will love them, care for them, and watch out for them. But ultimately, they are God's. We are entrusted with them for a time."

"It gave me a lot of peace," Danny shared with me, "to remember that Titus is God's. I don't feel so helpless when I hold this perspective."

This was a game-changer for Danny. His eyes were opened to a new way of looking at our circumstances. It was a perspective that became eternally focused. But I couldn't say the same for me. I reeled at the fact that he could even verbalize that our son could *die!* I mean, things had been rough. But I thought he was being a tad dramatic.

"Do you really think Titus could die?" I questioned him. "People live with seizures all the time. I'm sure once we get to the bottom of this, we can get him back to normal."

"We'll see, Bek. But people die from seizures and, I don't know, I just feel like he could." Danny's intuition made me uncomfortable. And I didn't believe it.

Even in my chaotic world, I perceived myself to have control. I just needed the right formula to make things work properly again. This whole idea of holding my children loosely as a gift from God didn't work for me. I had birthed this child and he was supposed to grow up and grow old! I couldn't even fathom being asked to release my son.

I put on my brave face again.

We would find a way to fix this.

BLOG ENTRY: MARCH 2015

My head is being held up in between my hands. I feel so deeply that I'm starting to go numb and can't feel anymore...

I crumble to the floor in the bathroom, sobbing, pleading for my boy back...

I scream at God, cursing Him, throwing a temper tantrum that resembles my teenage years...

I just can't. Not anymore. No more strength. No more.

This week, my joy was stolen. I wasn't sure how to get it back, either. I cried into my husband's arms and expressed my frustration at the fact that hope was gone. It's been a rough week. A really rough week.

Titus continued to seize so much these past few days that he just hasn't functioned. He attempts, and we still see a smile here and there, but he struggles too. I'm sad at how he needs to go lie down throughout the day because he is so exhausted from the seizures. I'm sad at how he has a hard time walking on his own or eating on his own. I'm sad at how his big, gorgeous eyes are only ever half-open anymore. Every night, when he lies down to sleep, my stomach goes in knots, afraid of what we may encounter that night or the next day.

And then my mind keeps going. I'd think about what we would encounter if he was hospitalized. I told God I didn't have strength for a hospitalization right now. I'd think about the therapies needing to get started to help him and I told God I didn't have strength for more therapy sessions and doctor's appointments right now. I'd think about his future and his inability to be independent that may carry into his adult years and I told God I don't have the strength for that right now.

No, you don't... He said.

I start to cry... again. How can I write about joy and hope and heart change when I feel this way?

And in my desperation God speaks to my heart, like He always does, meeting me in my despair.

Daughter, all you need strength for is to lay your head on that pillow and go to sleep.

I breathe. Just today. I only need strength for today. I only need strength for right now. And He has given me that.

"Give your entire attention to what God is doing right now and don't get worked up about what may or may not happen tomorrow. God will help you deal with whatever hard things come up when the time comes." Matt. 6:34 (The Message)

Guess what happened next?

Titus was admitted into the hospital for an estimated ten-day stay. I've grown to hate these stays. But when the neurologist came in to our clinic visit and said he felt it best to send Titus right over to the hospital, something happened inside me. I felt strong. We could do this; Danny and I. God was giving us enough for that moment. Because that's all we needed. Just today...

Thanks for listening...

Bekah

NOTES

_____

_____

_____

_____

_____

_____

_____

_____

_____

_____

_____

_____

_____

_____

_____

_____

_____

CHAPTER TWO

A STOLEN PRESENT

shrank down on the kitchen floor, partially from exhaustion, but mostly because I was broken and my legs didn't want to work anymore. Funny how the broken heart can affect all things physical. I've met this kitchen floor before in this way, and the familiarity broke me loose. It flooded out. I grieved a past gone far too quickly where a once healthy boy lived.

I feared a future that loomed dark and hopeless as we fought an unknown monster who wouldn't relent. I resented a present life that couldn't be lived in because of the grief of the past and fear of such a dark future. Watching TV in the other room were two boys who needed their mama, one of them greatly affected by seizures which medication couldn't control, the other a baby boy who adored his big brother.

I shouted as loudly as one can through the words of a desperate journal entry.

"I am struggling, God! I see the toys sitting on the shelves— toys that used to be played with all day long, grabbed by my sweet boy's long slender hands, imagination wild, eyes alert and attentive, immersed in what he was acting out. Now they sit and he just sits, exhausted by the fight of mis-firings in his brain. How can this be okay? How can this be good? I can't even bring myself to think of the suffering he endures. God, I've gotta get a hold of this... you have to help me. Because right now, well, right now I feel cheated, damaged, beyond repair, totally shattered and broken. I want to hear 'Mama' again! To see his enthusiastic responses to life! To watch him light up at each new adventure. I want him to live! **How is this living?!***" I yelled through the words spilling out angrily over the white-lined page."*

"You say all things work together for good. My heart so rejects this being the best way to accomplish good. You are going to have to help me today. God, I need to see You. I need a renewed belief in You because right now, all I see is sorrow. Don't leave me here, God. Don't You dare."

My recent kitchen floor meeting brought me to the awareness that this brave face of mine was no longer working out. I had come to the end of myself and my faith was engaging in a deeply spiritual battle. All my life I had grown up learning about a God who weaves everything together for good. A God who loves us and wants good things for us. All my life, my mom spoke the verse Jeremiah 29:11 (NLT) over me.

"For I know the plans I have for you," says the Lord. "They are plans for good and not for disaster, to give you a future and a hope."

As I grew through my teenage years, she continued to speak these words of truth, life and blessing over me. But this truth I'd grown up learning and had experienced no longer described the same God I was experiencing in my present reality.

In my pleading, there was a gentle prodding. A prodding that said perhaps there was more to this picture than I could possibly know. And perhaps, the most life-giving, good thing I could do right now was to peer into what was right in front of me. I glanced at the custom quote I had put over my door nine months before, when we moved into our home after making a cross-country transition from Illinois to southern California. The quote read, *Today, you get to be part of the greatest story ever told.*

I had no idea how wrong I had it as I wallowed in all the pain of the future. I had no idea just how drastically my perspective needed to shift. The danger of not shifting my perspective? I was at risk of not only losing my son, but losing every moment I had with him.

My mind flashed back to a conversation I had with my husband the year prior. Titus was getting ready to head to his first day of preschool. He was three. And just like a good mama does, my mind jumped to Kindergarten and all the worries we could meet when we got there. My husband as my audience, I wondered out loud what Kindergarten would be like for Titus and quickly followed it with about ten things I was legitimately worried about!

I still remember Danny grinning at me.

"Well," he began, "I learned in Kindergarten that crayons taste disgusting, recess was the best part of the day, and you could get away with just about anything as long as you timed it right."

He went on, "And in first grade, I learned that it was funny to blow spit wads through straws."

And on, "And in second grade, I learned that throwing rubber erasers at girls earned detention." He paused and grinned. "Do you want me to keep going?"

"No, please—for the sake of all bad case scenarios that are running through my mind, please *stop!*" I laughed.

And yes, I got the message he was sending. That particular day was the first day of preschool. It wouldn't help anyone to worry about two years down the road. I loved my son so much, I wanted him to be successful in all he did. But my worry didn't gift us anything. Instead, it used future what-ifs to rob the present. My presence was needed right then and there, celebrating the first day of preschool.

My flashback served as a reminder that this was a lesson I needed to re-learn. I needed to walk into that room where my boys sat together in a recliner watching *Cars*; Titus holding his Mater plush, pushing the button to make him talk over and over again. I began to breathe out a prayer: "Let me see your beauty, God." Breathe. Pray. Repeat. My hands pushed off the tile kitchen floor as I stood. I set my journal down on the counter, surrendering again with a plea to see what I couldn't see on my own and climbed in next to my boys and their world of the redneck tow truck and red celebrity racecar.

It became a discipline for me, in every moment with my boys, whether my eyes were laughing or crying, to open them to see what was before me. I discovered such beautiful gifts that were no longer stolen by the discoloration of the past or the fuzziness of the future. No, instead my present moments were held in perspective of past and future. The past proved to me I had no idea what was coming next. It also proved to me that it passed by without my say and the only choice I got to make was whether I would engage in life or watch it slip by, worried by every little thing that may or may not happen. The future proved to me to always be different than what I expected. No matter what scenarios I played out in my mind with well thought-out execution, it would look different. And so, my best gift to my future would be to pay attention to the present.

Here was where I was learning. *Here* was where I was growing. *Here* was where the Lord had me. *Here* was where I could seek His beauty and declare thankfulness for it. And in that thankfulness, find joy and peace. Knowing that He was doing far more than I could imagine with this small story of ours gave me the courage to search for the extraordinary among the mundane. And to be here, always right here.

NOTES

CHAPTER THREE

A FORGETFUL PEOPLE

love the Old Testament of the Bible. I love the stories and the redemption woven all throughout it as God points His people to a
Redeemer who would come to save them. The miracles God works
to preserve the bloodline of Christ proves His perspective is big and
eternal. And as I read these epic stories of floods and famines, proph-
ecies and rescues, I am hit with this same revelation over and over. We
are a forgetful people. People were forgetful of God's goodness and
promises in the Old Testament, and we still are today.

Conviction hits.

Yep, I'd forgotten. My little story—the role I played as Bekah the
mom—had taken over my entire perspective and my lower story was
the lens through which I saw life. It didn't look pretty through this set
of lenses. They had been chipped by hurtful words and offenses that

pelted me out of nowhere. They were dirty from the cloud of sorrow and pain for what Titus was forced to endure. They were splattered in selfishness, fear, and anger. And what I saw through them was hopelessness. Would I manage to pull myself out of this? Perhaps find some little DIY kit that could patch up and heal the dents, scratches, and chips this life has created? Hashtag the power of positive thinking?

It was a simple staff meeting that moved my heart to transformation, in a moment when my boss reminded us, "We need to remember what God has done." And then asked, "What has God done that you need to remember and celebrate right now?"

But all I could see was Titus, what he looked like when he had those terrible seizures and the fact that he was not healed, despite our faithful prayers asking for that very thing. As anger took over, I couldn't figure out how to share what God had done. We were all pondering what needed to be remembered, celebrated. I was sitting there, fury welling up, because I could think of plenty to be thankful for. Indeed, there were many moments to celebrate. But there was this one giant looming thing He hadn't taken care of—my son's sickness.

Ironically, my phone rang just minutes after this question was asked. I looked down as my phone vibrated in my lap and excused myself. It was our babysitter. "Titus had a seizure and fell off the chair, hitting his head," she explained.

I sighed. "I'll be right there," I told her. When I came back to the table, I exchanged a knowing look with a couple of my coworkers. This wasn't the first time I had been called out due to seizures. It had been happening more and more frequently. I leaned down to whisper to the junior high pastor that I had to head home. She promised to relay the message and asked that I keep her updated.

As soon as my feet hit the back stairwell leading to the parking garage, I ran. My boy needed me and I needed to hold him. I needed to see him and make sure he was okay. I climbed in the car and the fierce tears started. I shoved them away as I dialed my husband's phone to let him know the situation. After I hung up, promising to call him as soon as I got home, I centered my eyes on the road ahead. And my mind wandered back to the conversation happening at that staff meeting table.

"We need to remember what God has done," he had stated. *Need.* *Need.* It was a survival tool. I felt the fear pulsing through my brain, sending signals to fight or run away. But another voice fought through the fog of fear. *Child, remember.*

On that drive home, God sent me a lifeline. It took on the identity of faithfulness, but I couldn't fully see it for what it was until I looked back. As He wooed me to the past where I could clearly see His handiwork, I found myself on the labor and delivery bed in Kankakee, Illinois, about to meet my youngest son, Ely.

The doctor tells me to push, so I do. I'm so ready to see my son, it's been a long night and day. As I look forward, laboring exhaustive love, a look of shock comes across my doctor's face. Inside me something snapped. It all happened so fast, I had no idea what was going on, until I hear, "Oh my gosh, the cord was really tight around his neck. It wasn't allowing us to pull him out until your cord snapped away from your placenta allowing him to be delivered. I've never ever seen that happen." Ely was quickly rushed over to receive oxygen, his silence ripped through the room. Danny paced. I cried. The doctor kept mumbling, "I've never seen that happen. I've never seen that happen."

We waited for words of comfort that our son was going to be okay. We didn't get any. We heard no cries, the quiet our newest sense of torture. Finally, I hear my son's vocals fill the room and the nurse looks at me, smiles and says, "He's going to be okay, Mom." Tears of relief poured even faster. God cut the cord. He protected my son and cut the cord.

And then another remembering...

It was Christmas Eve. Danny and I were headed up to Comer's Children's Hospital in Chicago with Ely. It had been a tough road for him in his first months of life. He was slated for surgery due to malrotation of the intestines, which was discovered on an upper GI test performed just a couple weeks before. I'd never heard of it, but quickly learned it could not reverse on its own and was very dangerous. But when diagnosed, it was completely fixable. Leading up to that day, Ely had started throwing up the color green. He hadn't had a bowel movement in days. All signs pointed to a situation gone very bad. As we were sitting in the waiting room for the medical team to take one last look at his intestines before sending us to the surgeon, he had the biggest blow out diaper I had ever seen. Right there in the waiting room. Awesome. We frantically tried to reign in the scene before us, as onlookers politely tucked their faces into their shirts.

We paused in the frantic hustle to look at each other. "He pooped!" we celebrated. That was a big deal! We headed in to the room where they ran a second upper GI test. After looking over the findings, the doctor reported, "We see significant reflux, but no malrotation of the intestines. Surgery is not necessary at this time!"

My first reaction was that the first doctor got the test wrong. But then our pediatrician tells us, at a follow-up visit, that she saw both tests and there was malrotation and then there wasn't!

She had never in her twenty-plus years of practicing, seen mal-rotation reverse like that. She called Ely her miracle baby. We made our way home for Christmas thanking God for the way He showed up.

I'd like to think God knew we needed these gifts. He knew when broken circumstances surrounded us, we would need a lifeboat to pull us out of the storm and give us a reason to look up once again. On the drive home, the faithfulness of my Father filled me.

I arrived home to find my boys sitting together on the couch. The babysitter gave me a brief rundown. I thanked her and sent her home. I wasn't going anywhere. I was here to stay for the rest of the day. I checked in with Titus and Ely and called my husband. We avoided major injury this time. Thankfully, Titus seemed to be faring well after his latest episode. I sat down with my boys and grabbed an empty journal. Once I allowed my spiritual muscle of remembering to flex, it was ready to put in some work. I had more rememberings to scribble out.

It was as if I had tapped into a superpower. Instead of a fickle dance with circumstances, I was rooted in something deeper and bigger. I didn't have to side-step or bow out when my situation told me to. I could dive deep and hold firm and in that, I found clarity in the middle of broken.

I found deep truth in my conscious decision to remember and celebrate. When I took the time to look back, I saw a God consistent with His values and character. The circumstances that muddied my perspective cleared away when I reflected back. On that day and the days that followed, I began the regular practice of looking back, remembering, celebrating, and declaring gratitude.

The empty journal I had pulled out became my gratitude journal. Each page was dedicated to one thing I would praise God for. One thing I would celebrate that He had done. Places He had shown up. Gifts He had given us. Beauty He gave me the eyes to behold.

My list was simple. But that was the secret God was revealing to me. There was beauty everywhere and in all the little mundane things, celebrations waiting to be had.

My list began:

• Thankful for laughter
• Thankful for amazing teachers for my boys
• Thankful for a husband who will trim my kids' nails (I hate that job)
• Thankful for comfy clothes and a hot cup of coffee
• Thankful for beautiful flowers that my boys must reach out and touch each time we pass by them
• Thankful for lifelong friends, their silly texts, and the connections felt from afar
• Thankful for quiet moments in the car, a breeze blowing through the windows as I wait in the pickup line at school
• Thankful for Ely's enthusiastic "WOOOOW" at all things wondrous to his young eyes
• Thankful for my body's ability to carry Titus around the park and help him go down the slide and experience all that he once could do on his own
• Thankful for our single level home

My list went on and on. Each "Thankful" statement held a story of the goodness of God I desperately needed to remember.

One story of God's faithfulness and His promise to go before us was held in our small single-story condo. If you have ever been to Orange County, California, you know that single story homes are in the minority. When God called us from Illinois to California in 2014, Titus was four and Ely was one. At that time, Titus struggled with seizures, but was otherwise healthy. Danny and I flew out a month before we were to make the big move to look for a rental.

As the realtor took us through each prospect, it was hard to find a place well taken care of, in a good location, and affordable. I had my eye on a particular two-story condo in South County, but the upstairs loft had these abnormally wide-spaced rails. I could just see with my "worst-case scenario-ing" super-mom power, both my boys squeezing through those rails to plummet to the depths below. In every image, I searched for a way to save them. But, seeing as this was a worst-case scenario super power I was tapping into, a rescue was just not possible.

So, I took our top choice off the list. I couldn't do it. I couldn't live in the fear that my boys could fall through those rails at any moment. Our hunt continued. The realtor had put a small single-story condo on our list. It had no garage and was smaller than what we had in mind. We moved it to the end of the day as a "we'll see it, if there is time" option. As it turned out, we did have time. We stopped by the place, not expecting much.

We fell in love with it. It was homey, clean, in a wonderful neighborhood, and close to Danny's work. Sure, it was small. Maybe downsizing would be good for us. Both the boys would still have their own rooms, and despite no garage, we could see ourselves doing life in this cozy space. We sent the owner a completed application, a letter, and a picture of our young family of four.

She chose us and we moved in a month later. We acclimated quickly to our new space. It wasn't until several months after, I would see how God had gone before us in something as small as finding our new home. It happened to be the only single level home available to us in our price range. I thanked God on a daily basis for no stairs as Titus's seizures were unpredictable. We also had no idea that as our story unfolded there in California, we would need people. And those people were a mile down the road from our home at Journey Christian Church. They would enter our lives a little over a year after moving there.

Thank goodness I don't have to find the power to weave all things together for good or be worried about lining it all up just so. I don't have the foresight for that, but God does. We usually don't get to see His foresight until it becomes our hindsight. Which is why we must remember. We must look back and celebrate. We must declare thankfulness.

Even in those deep dark places where we felt robbed, we found, through thankfulness, we could gain.

We gained love.

We gained perspective.

We gained hope.

We gained joy.

NOTES

PART TWO

IT'S NOT GOOD NEWS

BLOG ENTRY: APRIL 2015

As I read a bedtime story to my son tonight, I couldn't keep back the tears. "Mama, what if I were a slimy smelly sea creature with seaweed hanging from my body?" asks the boy in the book. And his mama assures him she would love him for exactly who he was, slimy, smelly seaweed and all. "I love you, my wonderful child," she says.

I sat and pondered love. How do we use love to help those around us fly, to be a part of God's story the way He intends? As I was spending time just listening, God spoke this into my heart. "Love is: not holding someone to the impossible and fake standard of perfection the world holds them to, while simultaneously championing them to be the very best version of themselves. In this you give that individual a chance to live authentically in who I (God) have created them to be." I'll be honest. At first, I thought He was directing this to my heart because of how I needed to respond differently to my husband. And truthfully, I did need to hear it for that purpose. But over the last few weeks this has taken on a whole new meaning for me. I believe God gave this to me so I could hold on to it now when I've felt the most broken than I've ever felt before.

A year ago, I remember thinking I would surely break... snap at any moment. Danny and I were living in high alert mode as our son Titus had begun having seizures and wasn't responding well to medication. Our youngest, Ely, began having what the medical world called "ALTE's", apparent life-threatening episodes. Ely would have such a forceful spit up that it would clog his nose and throat leaving him unable to breathe or clear out the spit up on his own. Danny and I, countless times, suctioned him out, adrenaline pumping, working as fast as we could to save him from aspiration and ultimately, our worst fear—him dying.

As we faced one health challenge after another, there was always something we could do to help our children. We avoided a major surgery early on, but Ely eventually went in for a different stomach surgery. A successful fundoplication procedure stopped the dangerous episodes that had threatened him. Because he had also been designated "failure to thrive" as a result of not being able to keep down his food, he had a feeding tube put in during that surgery as well. Ely landed back on the growth chart shortly after. What a relief that was!

We've faithfully given Titus every medication the doctors have prescribed to control his asthma and allergies. We have diligently searched for answers to his seizures and what we could do, radical or traditional, to help him. We sought out every therapy and assessment he needed and diligently got him on an IEP. Along the way were promises this was just a difficult season and we would see improvement with time.

Our search for answers ended this week. Tuesday at 11:45 AM, to be exact. And we are left with the ability to do only one thing... Love. Titus was diagnosed with a rare genetic disease called late infantile NCL. It is progressive. It is fatal. There is no treatment and no cure. This disease will take our sweet boy away before he can experience being a teenager.

There isn't anything we can do to reverse the bad genes to heal him. Appointment after appointment this week confirmed the diagnosis. And I'm left feeling desperate, helpless, sad... so, so sad. I find myself saying to Titus over and over again, "I love you."

God has been speaking to me in my deep brokenness of an even deeper love. A love that enables Titus to be all he was meant to be, despite the obvious imperfections we see in this world. I want to champion and love my son like that.

This week I've become broken. More broken than I knew I could be. So broken I can't fix it and I'm overcome by it.

But... out of the broken comes love. An authentic, new eye-opening kind of love.

Oh, how I love and am loved.

Thanks for listening... And keep praying.

Bekah

CHAPTER FOUR

LOVE VS BITTERNESS

So there we were, a diagnosis in hand. It was in this moment I became keenly aware of something called anticipatory grief. A knowing that someday we were going to lose big time. And in that current moment, we were already losing our son. This monster that now had a name was stripping our son of his ability to walk, talk, eat, see, remember, laugh, and stomp like a dinosaur. And there we were, grieving.

As we woke up the day after the diagnosis, and the day after that and the day after that, we muddled through a million emotions. I had my camera out all the time, capturing every moment with my boys. When I watched Titus seize, drop straight to the ground, or throw something out of frustration because he was growing blind and couldn't see, my whole being ached, screamed out and cried. When I watched Titus and Ely giggling on the back patio playing like two brothers should, my whole being still ached, screamed out and cried. I grieved the good and the bad.

The good was so hard to watch. My eyes wanted to shut tight to pretend like I wasn't seeing it. Maybe that meant life would freeze and we wouldn't close in on the days when I wouldn't witness this brotherly relationship anymore. Yet, I also wanted to live with my eyes wide open. I didn't want to miss a single thing. I lived knowing each day could be the last I would hear a word, see an expression, or watch him play with his favorite toys. I knew any day could be our last chance to watch him walk to his brother and hug him and then wrestle him to the ground. Each sweet moment was met with laughter and tears, both on my face and in my soul. *"Don't miss this,"* my heart told me. *"Don't let this disease steal your joy, your moments, your soul."*

But oh, how I hated the bad. How I grew to hate this disease. I had never heard of it before. Batten Disease, the doctor had called it. Titus had been missing an important enzyme right from birth, myself and my husband passing along the same defective gene to our boy. It was a defective gene that had been silently carried, passed down generation to generation in both our families, completely unbeknownst to us. And now our son was the victim. As this important enzyme remained deficient and virtually nonexistent in his body, the waste in his cells began to build up, damaging them and eventually putting the cells to death. With no enzyme to clean the waste, there was no hope in stopping the horrific degeneration that would take place. My son would lose his ability to walk. To talk. To eat. To see. To breathe on his own. To cough. To learn. To remember. And it would take him away. Soon.

This disease was a thief. It was stealing from me. It was stealing from my boys, from my husband. I didn't realize until those aching moments, I had never even considered a life where my son wouldn't grow up. It had been a given to me that he'd become a man, have a family. It never crossed my mind that life could be different from that. And yet, people live in these broken places all the time. How blind I was to the hurting lives around me until I became a part of the clan. It was a slap in the face.

Our doctor encouraged us to reach out to the Batten Disease Support and Research Association for support. I emailed the director and she added me to the private support group page on Facebook.

She dared to write, "Please welcome Bekah, CLN2 Mom, to the group."

This followed with a bunch of folks leaving messages of "Welcome to the group!" "Glad you are here!"

I reeled. Mentally, my response was: *"Welcome to the group? Let's get one thing straight, folks. I DO NOT want to be here. I don't want to be a part of your lives. I don't want to even acknowledge you exist; much less acknowledge the struggle your child is going through. Because it means I acknowledge this battle exists in my own home. That the inevitable loss and the evil that is shredding my heart to pieces, is REAL. And I'm not ready."*

I signed off that Facebook group and refused to look at it for several weeks. I couldn't bring myself to Google Batten Disease. I couldn't think about the fact that my child received this disease through mutated genes that my husband and I both passed along, never knowing we were carriers. "It's not your fault," the geneticist said. "We all carry an average of 3 mutations on our genes. Yours just happened to be the same."

But my heart hurt. I'm supposed to protect my son, not harm

him. And if this was genetic, what about my little Ely? Surely the loss couldn't stretch that deep.

I suppose a part of me wanted to remain in that hurt place, feeling sorry for myself and angry. Perhaps even angry at God. But as I looked at Titus, I couldn't allow his life to culminate in bitterness and isolation. I loved him far too much for that. And bitter was the last word anyone would have used to describe Titus. In fact, he was often referred to as the *joy-boy*.

As news spread about Titus, an incredible support system rose up around us. A friend set up a GoFundMe account. Others set up meal trains and house cleaning services. My childhood besties organized a trip and flew in to just be with me for a few days. Neighbors checked on us, friends came over with their kids to play and life was brought in through our front door in countless other ways. Each individual who walked in and out of our broken household walked under that bold quote reminding us all that we were a part of a story bigger than ourselves. I felt so alive when I thought of how connected we all were to one big story—God's! In that deep muddy trench of fatal disease and loss, I watched love and life become interconnected in ways I had never witnessed before. I thought my life would be sucked dry to bitterness. But instead, I was being filled with love.

It was during a rare quiet moment in my house I found space to process what had been laid out before us. My thoughts were always running a million miles a minute. Some of them were like naughty children jumping all over the furniture—their only goal to wreak havoc, and others were trying to play hide and seek, poking their heads out for a moment giving me short glimpses but ducking out before I could fully understand. Many of my thoughts were on Titus, always on Titus. And other thoughts spent hours absorbed in what the future held for Ely. I dared to hope for a future for him and not a terminal diagnosis like his brother.

My thoughts moved through sorrow and pain to a deep and overpowering knowledge that all was not lost, hope was not gone, and victory was still won—yes, even over Batten Disease. As I sat in the quiet, allowing my thoughts an audience, processing each of them out, I realized the presence of evil was in front of me fighting with lies to take me down. I pulled out my battle weapon: my journal. And I begin to shape this conversation through the lined pages with evil himself, Satan.

"You think you've got this, don't you? You think you've got me down. I'll tell you what... it's been a valiant effort. And I'm broken, that's for sure. I'm scared. I'm angry. But that doesn't equal to being yours. Because I'll tell you what, Satan... you have to understand. I'm just the front lines in this little story, with a huge army behind me. When I go down, I will be pulled from the carnage and carried away from it. I will be cared for. I will be loved.

You have to take down my neighbor who stands by us and supports us in the daily grind.

You have to take down the friends who have also felt loss in parenting and have chosen to walk the same difficult road with us.

You have to take down the thousands who are praying for strength, peace, joy and healing.

You have to take down those who have chosen to support us

through donations and hugs.

You have to take down the first-grade class who made cards to encourage our son.

You have to take down a family who loves each other and stands by each other no matter what.

You have to take down moms (yeah, those are the worst ones) who intercede on our behalf through prayer, meal-making, grocery shopping, coffee drops to my front door and teary-eyed mama bear hugs.

And you wonder why I'm so strong; why I don't just fall? Because God has used my community to reinforce what I already know: that He loves us and we are not alone. And I will do the very same for anyone else who finds themselves battling on the frontlines in their story.

*Satan, you need to know... **you can't steal my joy.***"

In that moment, God made something abundantly clear to me. We weren't doing life alone. This level of community-lived life far exceeded my expectations. What I expected was for someone to hear our story and excuse themselves to find the exit. It's difficult. It's sad. It doesn't have a happy earthly ending. But that isn't what they did. They chose to join us. We were getting cards daily reminding us that there were others praying and interceding on our behalf, hurting with us, and encouraging us. Life had been overwhelming, but as people offered to go grocery shopping, make us meals, watch the boys, and just sit and listen when I needed to cry or talk, it all felt impossibly manageable. And the strangest thing happened in my heart. I had this ridiculous, unfettered joy in the daily moments of life. Joy! What business did I have being joyful?

Our life was dictated by moments of panic when Titus started seizing. Moments where he threw fits because he couldn't communicate like he used to and no one understood him. Moments of tube cleanings and diaper changes. Moments of sleepless nights and pain I couldn't ease. Moments of guilt as I tried to parent both my children while one required the majority of my time. Moments of failure as I gave up a career path I never thought God would ask me to give up, simply because I couldn't do it all.

Yes, I had a choice in those moments. I could choose the root of bitterness. I could allow my heart to rage at what had been lost, at what I perceived myself to be cheated out of. Or, I could choose love. I could choose to see God for who He was, no matter my circumstances. In that place, I received the gift of clear perception, and I recognized gifts of beauty I couldn't have seen from a position of comfort or bitterness.

Because we were buried under such ugly brokenness, the beauty of God became all the more clear. The contrast was drastic. When I was comfortable, I wasn't looking for it. When I was bitter, I was blinded to it. But in those moments of looking up to His great story, I *lived* for His goodness. I *needed* His beauty. I needed His powerful love and redemption when there was no other way to survive.

NOTES

CHAPTER FIVE

LEAN ON ME

A s I continued to feel that tug to look back and remember, I saw how consistently the community gathered around us time and time again.

There is something about going through deep, treacherous waters *with* people. There is something about going through those same waters alone, too. One is true to our nature and how we were created to operate: in community. The other is dangerous. To live in isolation is to invite in lies. It is to get sucked deep into our own little story and lose sight of the Bigger Story at hand that we are all a part of. It is to move ourselves into the main role, forcing us to depend only on ourselves. Knowing my own limitations, weaknesses and impulsivities, that is a scary place to be—dependent on self.

In our minds, we have self-doubt, negative talk, and an abundance of judgement. In Genesis 2:18 (NLT), God said, "It is not good for the man to be alone." *God said.* If God said, and He's our creator, then we better pay attention.

This community thing has to go beyond nice exchanges with our neighbors when we are out in our driveways at the same time. It even has to go beyond sitting in church with others week to week. Community must have depth, because without depth, relationships slither away as soon as life gets difficult. While we may be hurt by those who run away when life's road gets rocky, more often than not, it is we who push people away or isolate ourselves to the point where those around us don't even know our struggle.

I grew up in a home that prioritized people and friendships. We always lived far from our grandparents and extended family. I remember holidays like Thanksgiving and Easter being spent with friends because we weren't able to be with family. I grew up with countless adopted grandparents, aunts, uncles, second moms and dads.

When I was in third grade, we had Grandparents' Day at our school. I had come home bummed because I didn't have a grandparent close by who could go celebrate this special occasion with me. I'm not sure how all the behind-the-scenes planning happened, but a lady in our church volunteered to be my adopted grandma and to go with me that day for the special event. I remember walking through Grandparents' Day with my head held high because I had a somebody and a somebody had me.

Another couple around my grandparents' age decided they were going to invest in my brother and me. The details of our time together are blurry, but what is burned into my memory is how loved I felt in their presence. I felt chosen, and oh, how I cherished and loved them in return.

In my teenage years, a woman chose to invest her time in a handful of us crazy girls. Drama was ever prevalent. I still remember her speaking love over me as I felt betrayed, hurt, and lost in the middle of that drama.

My community didn't stop when I grew up and moved away. As my husband and I transitioned into our own lives and began our parenting journey, I watched an entire slew of new folks gather around us.

Two ladies, who I will cherish forever, loved on our boys every single week in the nursery as they grew from chubby babies to active toddlers.

I remember the individuals who came around Titus when he became difficult, allowing him room and space, giving him love and gentle spiritual direction.

I remember meal trains for days, friends running to pick up prescriptions, and adopted grandmas and grandpas coming over to help me with our bedtime routine when Danny was out of town for work.

I think about how blessed we have been to be able to prioritize date nights because God always provided people to love and care for our boys.

I think about the random acts of kindness from our people that ranged from In-N-Out Burger® drop offs, lawn mowing, and snow blowing our driveway to driving hundreds of miles to just be with us for surgeries and procedures.

I think of how interconnected our communities were; how vast they went beyond our little story. As our needs grew and we moved state to state, the amazing connection of God's family would follow us around in miraculous ways.

When we heard Titus's diagnosis for the first time, our next reaction (after slamming into devastation) was that we needed to be with our people. We put out an SOS call to our entire family. On April 19, 2015, we decided to take our boys to Disneyland for the first time. In the midst of life stripped away, we declared life lived. But we didn't want to be there alone—we wanted our community. You wouldn't believe the number of people who rallied, from Washington, Nebraska, Idaho, and all over California, to come be with us with a mere twelve days' notice.

Disneyland day fell on my husband's birthday. We were there to make memories and declare victory over Batten Disease. We marched in with thirty-one members of our extended family. All across the world, it became "Yellow Shirt Day" to support Titus, whose favorite color was yellow. As we traipsed through Disneyland, cherishing giggles on the train, meeting characters, and spending time with our loved ones, we received notification after notification of individuals from all over declaring joy alongside us as they wore yellow.

Through all of this, we were flexing our spiritual muscle to receive. Yes, that is a spiritual muscle, and it's one so many of us overlook and even look down on! We think we are here to help and serve others, but we must be strong, independent, and self-sufficient. These seemingly admirable traits drive us away from the foundation of our relationship with God. When we refuse to receive, we push away the very essence of our need for Him.

As we received, we were blessed to abundance. But that blessing wasn't just ours to hold. It spread through the hearts and souls of those serving us. In turn, they received beautiful, soul-nourishing gifts. We cannot miss how important it is to receive.

When we choose to receive, we are more equipped to give. Our family could deliver the message of hope and joy because we were given those very things. These qualities couldn't come out of us in and of ourselves. They had to be sourced from the very One who created hope and joy because He *is* hope and joy. Because we are created in God's image, we are image-bearers of hope and joy for each other. God has built lifelines into community!

But community is messy. It always has been because of our nature to lean toward self-preservation and self-interest. Inevitably, we find ourselves in places of hurt by each other. And this is exactly what evil wants—to foil the plan so community loses its power.

But in the mess is where God transforms us. As we hear Him calling to us, correcting us, modeling for us His way, we can once again invite Him and others back in to our hearts. We can do this life exactly as it was meant to be done—together. May we all actively participate on both sides of giving and receiving, putting God's love on display for this world to see.

NOTES

CHAPTER SIX

A DESPERATE PERSPECTIVE SHIFT

I looked at my son and wanted to cry. Our days were numbered and I really didn't want to spend them blubbering along. He was worth more than that. I had to find a way to help him truly live, not just survive day to day. As his abilities were stripped away and his body started to fail him in many ways, I fought hard to give him as much freedom as I safely could.

His physical therapist helped us get him onto an adaptive bike. It literally held up his entire torso, buckled him in with what looked like an 11-point harness system, and strapped his feet into the pedals. I used a handle on the back to push and steer. His feet rotated with the pedals as I moved him. He could actually bike! This was good for his muscles, and for our souls. We got out in the beautiful southern California sun every single day we could to bike around the neighborhood. Although Titus was losing his sight quickly and could no longer see other than shades of light against dark, he could hear! He could hear me talking to him as I pushed him along. He could hear the birds. He could hear the soft breeze blowing through the trees and he could smell the flowers. He could tell when someone else was near and saying hello, and he could hear kids laughing, balls bouncing and barbecues sizzling. I often closed my eyes (when it was safe to do so) along with Titus because I wanted to know what he was experiencing. From my limited perspective, it felt like his experiences had been stolen from him. Deeply. What kind of life was that?

It was on one of those walks, though, where I experienced a major perspective shift. I learned that blindness was indeed a big problem. Blindness stole experiences, the ability to see beauty, to identify things we would declare our favorites. Yes, it was a big problem indeed.

But in my discovery, I realized blindness was not a problem for my son. True blindness isn't physical, it's spiritual. And it was a plague that haunted me. So often in life, we believe we already know what "good" looks like. We think we know what "whole" looks like. And when something doesn't match up with our definition, we defend against it. We make it out to be criminal. To be wrong. To be avoided at all costs.

When you come to an intersection of life where you believe it should go one way, but there are construction cones and blockades that only allow you to take the other direction, you have to change your plans—quickly. Life had taken me down another road. I needed to pay attention to it rather than think about what it would be like on the road I had wanted to turn on. To live in that space wishing for another way, fed bitterness to my soul. It stole away my ability to be thankful for what I did hold in front of me. I was blinded by shadows of fear. I was blinded by my injustice over what life took away. I took my trust and held it tight, not gifting it to anyone or anything. If I did extend the hand of trust, who or what would come to crush it next?

This truth began washing over me as I walked Titus around the lake, his eyes unseeing but still beautifully blue, long lashes falling over his lids. How I ached at what he was enduring, and yet, right now, he didn't seem to be suffering. Perhaps there was another way to see life as we knew it. Perhaps there was more beauty to be found than what I believed was there all along. But what did it take to see such beauty?

Matthew 10:37-39 (NLT) came to mind: "If you love your father or mother more than you love me, you are not worthy of being mine; or if you love your son or daughter more than me, you are not worthy of being mine. If you refuse to take up your cross and follow me, you are not worthy of being mine. If you cling to your life, you will lose it; but if you give up your life for me, you will find it."

That was when I realized: All along, it hadn't been about an extreme God who puts His thumb in our back and demands that we follow a list of rules, regulations, and allegiances. This was about a God who says, *"Don't let this world blind you! See me! Look to me! When you look up, Daughter, you will see my faithfulness, my love, my grace, my purpose, my redemption, my victory! When you look up, Daughter, and follow me, you will find eyes to truly see. You will find a purpose worthy of giving your life for, because in it, you will find life itself."*

I soaked in what my heart was hearing as it took over for my ears. But the days that followed felt dark, and even as I began to sink into this truth, the daily existence of death in my house had me in its desperate grip often.

It was on another sleep-deprived fall night in our small condo home, a tiny space in the vastness of Orange County, California, when I knew I couldn't do this anymore. Those sleepless nights had become quite common in our house. I was clutching Titus close to my chest, gathering his long legs into my petite lap. At just five years of age, he was nearly as tall as me. The tile floor was cold, the room dimly lit by a lamp. My younger son slept peacefully in the room across the hall, my husband attempting to get a few hours of sleep in our room so he could function at work in the morning. I had been up more nights with Titus than I could count. The doctor had urged me to get a night nurse, but something in my heart hurt when I thought of a stranger caring for my son's needs in the dark of the night. On this particular night, Titus was in great distress. His cry went from a soft, mournful wail to a shrill yelp of pain, and then back into a mournful cry again. I could not calm him down.

As Titus cried out in pain and mourning, I tried medication, singing, rocking, distracting. But nothing worked to ease this bout of suffering. It was in that moment I suddenly became angry. As I held him, I could feel my body shaking. I was tense everywhere, unable to even catch a breath. I was so furious at this disease for what it was doing to us, to my boy. In that moment, my mama heart could no longer see Titus. I was blinded by an all-consuming hatred for this disease.

As I started to rock a little harder and my body shook, I realized I had to set Titus down and walk away. My anger was too present and I was so tired I couldn't think rationally anymore. As I walked away and heard him cry, knowing I couldn't care for him the way he needed me to, my soul, full of guilt and shame, but also blame screamed out to God. Someone needed to pay for this, because it wasn't fair.

In my rage, I cursed out in anger and flipped God off as I screamed at him, "What is happening? *And where are you?*" In that moment, I didn't see beauty in ugly places. I didn't feel redemption in our pain. Joy was the furthest thing from my mind. I didn't know who to trust or where to go for help. I was utterly broken.

As Christians, we like to say, "God will work all things for good."

"God has a plan for everything."

"God won't give you more than you can handle."

All those niceties I grew up hearing in the religious community crumbled away. I could not merge a good God who would just pat my head and say, "It's okay Daughter, I have a plan for these circumstances" with a God that would allow this horrific disease. As I raged at Him, an image flooded my mind. Everything else around me went quiet and dark. I curled up in a ball with tears spilling from my eyes.

The image that had taken over my entire sight and awareness was a picture of a man hung up on a cross. His head was drooped, the air gone out of His lungs. His skin was gaping open and ripped apart from being beaten. Actual nails were driven through His limbs. And there was so much blood. I felt myself nod at this image as my heart fell into the brokenness I was drowning in. I whispered out loud, "Yes, exactly. That kind of brokenness." My voice broke.

I was in this emotional free-fall waiting to hit the bottom, and when I arrived, there was this man on a cross. I thought I'd be alone down there, but I wasn't. He was there. There was no patting my head in a condescending way, no reasoning away my pain or telling me to get over it or to rise above. Rather, I began to see Jesus from an angle I had never understood before. In that moment I realized He was utterly broken and beaten, and given in to complete brokenness—*death*, the same brokenness my child was facing—so that in our brokenness He could be enough. He could say, *"I know Daughter. I am here, too."*

Talk about an "I've lived through it" kind of empathy. Nothing changed in my circumstances, but suddenly I felt so much Love. And yes, I mean capital L—Love. This wasn't a trump card God was trying to play on me to 'one-up' my story. He wasn't playing the comparison game. In that moment, it was validating Love that He was willing to fully feel and experience the brokenness we experience in this life. I gathered myself back up, knowing the pieces I picked up would never go back together the same way again. But I wasn't holding them in my small hands anymore. As I picked them up, I surrendered each one of them to Him. He was holding them for me with this tender care that said, *"No matter how heavy these things are, I will journey this with you. I will hold all of this and I will never leave."*

In broken and safe surrender, I walked back into my son's room, where his cries still echoed off the walls. The small lamp was still on in the corner and I could see shadows dancing across the walls. Because my Jesus had gone to complete brokenness with me, I climbed in to bed next to my son, held him, and was able to join him in his brokenness. We both calmed in the presence of the one who I called "Great Love" in that moment. My eyes were opened and I saw my son, not the disease. The disease had lost its victory in my soul-surrender to Jesus, who knew exactly what I felt. My mama heart was filled with love for Titus, no longer taken over by hate of our circumstances. My perspective shift as I became unblinded felt incredibly counter cultural. I was almost afraid to speak it out loud. To say, "Okay, God, if my son dies from this disease, I can still say it is well with my soul." But from deep within, I truly believed that could be possible. And, in believing that, I was living in truth more than I ever had. Because not even death could overcome my God and because of that, my son was safe with Him.

In that broken place was joyful victory. And death, while still shadowing us in this world, had just been defeated.

BLOG ENTRY: MAY 2015

Life as we know it is changing, fast. Each time we adjust, change happens and we have to adjust again. We are living in a stark reality that there is a timeline on my son's life... it isn't assumed, it is a fact. And the fact is it's too short. We are supposed to live long, die old, experience great things! Titus should be able to play in his first soccer game, graduate, get married, and be a dad! That is really living! Right?

This disease has stolen a lot from us in a short time. I find myself in tears over the "lasts" we've experienced that I didn't even know were "lasts." The last time I would hear my son proudly state that his name is "TITUS!", the last time I would see him run to the park ahead of me, the last time I would know for a fact that he saw me smile at him, the last time I would hear him say "love you." As this change has happened, I've had to figure out new ways to relate to my son. His vision is almost gone. How do I help him still see? What does that even mean? He is going to go the rest of his days blind. Does that mean he will miss out on the beauty this life offers?

And then I read this out of One Thousand Gifts, by Ann Voskamp: "The only place we need see before we die is this place of seeing God, here and now." [1]

My son doesn't have to score a goal to fully live. He doesn't have to live to be ninety-two with grandkids and great-grandkids to fully live. My son doesn't have to be able to see everything around him to fully live. My son is fully living here and now, and I know this because I see his spirit. I see his joy. Joy does not have a physical prerequisite to be able to experience it. We do not have to physically see God to know He's here and working. We see Him through our spirit.

This aha moment has given me new eyes, too. I no longer walk blindly through the day, doing my momma thing, only to have my eyes opened by some majestic landscape or some huge miraculous happening. My eyes are always open. And so are Titus's. We breathe in the daily beauty, the smiles, cuddles, hugs. We breathe in encouraging words from others, the times we play fetch with our dog, when we go outside on a walk, or times when we simply lay still. Through all of that and more, I find reasons to be thankful. Out of thankfulness for all God has done and continues to do, I find joy.

We aren't operating in bucket list mode anymore. I don't think to myself, "Someday when we do 'xyz', we'll really be living." That is a dark path for me to walk. Instead, I choose to see life through the eyes of joy in the here and now. Through the eyes of thankfulness in the here and now. We don't ever completely grasp what God has done and is doing until we learn how to live in this way. How to see through new eyes.

Today, I saw my son's spirit as he pursed his lips and spat, egging me on to do a giant raspberry on his tummy. I see his spirit in the way he calms as I hold him. And in the way he pounds his arms up and down to feel his world and how he still laughs at his brother because he just knows what Ely is doing. And when my son can no longer show any of this through his physical body, I will still pick him up and dance with him. I will still sing to him, pray with him, hold him. I know that he will still see God despite his physical limitations. Today, I choose thankfulness and joy, here and now. Gifts I can only see through new eyes.

Thanks for listening...

Bekah

NOTES

CHAPTER SEVEN

OH, COME ON!

It was summer vacation time. Our destination was Idaho to see all the family. It was special and necessary to make that trip as Titus continued to change quickly. We had just celebrated his 5th birthday. How very different the celebration looked from the year before. My sweet boy had become wheelchair bound, was tube fed and blind. Never in our wildest dreams did we picture year five looking like that.

We drove from Southern California up to Southeastern Idaho, conquering the ride in one day. What we didn't anticipate was that an hour down the road, our brand-new minivan would blow a tire and cause us to sit on the side of the road and then in a tire shop, prolonging our productivity on the one-day drive. My maiden name was Murphy. I've never gotten away from the curse of belonging to a family dictated by a law. (I joke. Kind of.)

As we drove into Idaho and found ourselves about forty-five minutes away from Grandma and Grandpa Murphy, our clock turned 11:00 pm. We were all tired, but in otherwise good spirits. As we drove through another small town with a gas station and convenience store as the prime real estate, we noticed some fireworks going off in the distance. We rolled down the windows, the late summer night still warm. There on the side of this back-country road, we found a small crowd of folks in a gravel parking lot where they had gathered to set off fireworks. Before each firework, the announcer turned on a microphone and described what firework would go off next. Silence followed. Then a boom and flashes of color. Silence. Announcer. Silence. Boom. Repeat. It was one of the worst fireworks shows I'd ever seen but something about it made us stop. It was small town charming. We rolled into the parking lot, rolled the boys' windows down all the way, and likely became the only out-of-town spectators.

We should've been on the road finishing our trip, but the happenings of our life in the months prior to this night caused us to stop often and pay attention to the moments we were in. And boy, was it worth it when we did pay attention.

From the back rose a soft giggle. Then a shrill of excitement. Tears welled up in my eyes and a smile lit across my face as I looked at my husband to see if he had noticed too. Titus, our blind son, was delighted at the sound of the fireworks. As giggles rolled out of his throat, the image of his wide-open smile burned into my mind. An unerasable memory. Right there, in the most unassuming town, in the unpaved parking lot of a convenience store, with a small crowd of people who likely didn't expect anyone new to show up at 11:00 at night—a blind son, a brokenhearted set of parents, and a baby brother found incredible joy. And that was how we started our vacation.

As we made our way from one set of grandparents to the next set across the state, we found ourselves waking up to an otherwise normal morning on June 25. My husband went out with his dad for some morning errands, and the rest of us were relaxing and enjoying conversation. My sister-in-law had even driven down from Washington with her son for a couple of days to see us.

My phone rang—a California number. I answered, and on the other end I heard the voice of our genetic counselor. We had met with her just weeks ago after the confirming diagnosis of Batten for Titus and had discussed the importance of getting Ely tested as well. We had gone through the motions and sent his test in, not expecting results for another week or two.

"I was calling with the results of the Batten CLN2 gene test for Ely. Would you like to talk now or come in when you get home?" she asked.

Are you kidding? I thought. "Now is fine."

"Are you sure?" she asked. And my heart sunk. Why would she ask if the news was good? I slipped into the other room away from the commotion of family and sank down onto the only seat I could find, my mother-in-law's exercise bike.

"Yes, I'm sure," I said. I felt my throat constrict. My nose started to tickle from the tears I was holding back. I knew what she was about to say, the words she would speak into being.

She sighed. Not a careless, annoyed sigh. One that held heavy news that she herself didn't even want to acknowledge.

"I'm so sorry, Rebekah, but Ely has Batten too."

A whispered "no" made its way past the growing lump in my throat. It couldn't be. Ely had overcome so much in his short life already, and he was thriving! I heard him in the other room making everyone laugh, as he always did. My chest constricted, fighting against the crushing weight that had just been delivered to me. How does heaviness like that make it through cyberspace, anyway? I maintained what voice I could to ask, "So what now?"

Time has made this part of my memory a bit foggy as I don't remember much of what she said. Mostly because there was no hope offered. No fix. Just an offer to consult if we chose to have more of our own children.

I hung up the phone and without checking in with anyone, I bolted out the front door. To this day, I'm not exactly sure where I had intended to go, but I didn't get far before my knees hit the cement walkway, my hands thrust out to stop my sudden collapse. Grief poured out of my soul in an otherworldly wail. I literally felt like my youngest son had just been killed. And that wasn't far from the truth. He was inside playing, a healthy almost-two-year-old, walking, talking, learning, and developing just like his cousin who was the same age. To imagine something wrong, something lurking inside his body waiting to take him away just like his brother—it was horror.

I felt tender arms wrap around me. My sister-in-law had followed me out, realizing something was wrong. I uttered four words before sorrow swallowed my voice again: "Ely has it, too."

I buried my face in my hands and let the Lord of the weary, Lord of the weak, Lord of the mourning have it. In my wailing, I cried out to Him because we had already been given too much. This broke me. I managed to think of my next step—to call my husband. I tried to speak the words out loud to him, but each time I spoke them, grief whooshed in, making every syllable an unintelligible wail.

"Calm down. What?" He tried to understand.

And again, "Bekah, I don't know what you are saying."

I handed the phone to his sister and asked her to tell him. He responded, "I'm on my way home." When he arrived, we held each other in disbelief. Then we began to do what we had just done two months earlier. We put in phone calls to our family and friends, letting them know the news. Our son, Ely, would be forced to fight this battle too.

What does one do when delivered fatal news for not just one, but both children? I held them tight. I watched everything they did, taking it in as best I could. I loved hard. I drank Frappuccinos® with my family, laughed, and committed it all to treasured memory.

And then I would disappear to the bathroom and cry.

Just days after this fatal news, we celebrated Ely's 2nd birthday with the family there in Idaho. As he opened his singing cards (because those have always been his favorite), all of us with our phones out capturing pictures and videos, he sang a gusto duet of "Let It Go" with Elsa. We all cheered and laughed and clapped, which made him go back for more accolades for his singing talents. My youngest son, the clown, always wanted to make people laugh. I still remember where I was standing for his first concert. The grandparents were all huddled around the circular table where Ely sat. I stood just behind the grandparents watching my son display joy and love in really big ways. I fought back tears. I didn't want this to be a sad moment. But, oh, how I wanted to protect this little one from the storm up ahead. I wanted to see what he would be capable of and how God would use him as he grew up through the years.

That night, I tried to go to bed with everyone else. To no one's surprise, sleep would not find me that night. I got up and sat on the bathroom floor, journal in hand, asking God to find me there. To pour His Spirit on me and show me how to survive this.

And He did just that.

I can see it all... the way his eyes light up all blue and the widow's peak defines his face so distinctly. How he stands fearlessly in the water, splashing, jutting out his jaw just slightly. Throwing water over himself in a shimmery, watery arc, glistening in the sun. The way he accidentally splashes water right into his face, tries his best to wipe it off, and then goes back for more. That's my Ely! Adventurous, fearless, mischievous, curious, joyful.

I watched his grandma, grandpa, aunt, and daddy look on with love, being sure to cheer for him on command, and Ely will command! They took pictures, video, anything to capture the moment... to make sure we didn't miss it, wouldn't forget it.

Nothing spirals you into living in the moment quite like the type of news our family has had to hear. And today we had to hear it again. Our baby, our Ely, is also affected by this monster we call Batten Disease. He will follow in the same path as his brother. As I spoke to our genetic counselor today in our two-minute phone call, my first word was a devastated, "No...", and next, "What now?"

Both of them, Lord? BOTH OF THEM, LORD?

I'm thrown into a spiral of deep sorrow, collapsing on the sidewalk in front of my in-laws' house, sobbing. My sister-in-law was immediately by my side, only down to visit us for one full day... this just happened to be the day. I called my husband to break the news. He rushed back to the house, and we began to relive what we just did two and a half short months ago with our oldest. Our worst nightmare. And I still have that question.

What now?

Oh, the amount of loss we are experiencing in a single moment is too much, crippling in the cruelest ways, tearing all control from our fingertips.

What now?
The tears don't stop... happy moments, sad moments, they all tweak at the heart the same way.

What now?
The lies running through my mind, telling me I must not have what it takes to parent a teenage boy. The pain I feel when I see other children achieve what my children never will.

What now?

The only answer resounding in my heart is this moment now. Right now. This... this now.

This... where my son grabs his bottle and curls up next to me.

This... where he demonstrates his hard-headedness and throws a fit complete with hitting, screaming, and throwing himself to the ground, usually engaging in this behavior in a moment that ensures a larger audience than just my eyes.

This... where he growls "daaadaaa" every time daddy comes home from work.

This... when he snuggles his head into my neck as we dance around the room singing our bedtime song.

This... when he grabs his shoes off the rack, showing us he's ready for an adventure, any adventure.

This... his love for people and the way he can engage with each individual with a twinkle in his eye.

This is where I live. I've been living in "this-land" for a while now. And what is being defined in a clearer way all the time as I occupy this state of mind is thankfulness. Not the polite "Thank you so much" kind of thankfulness, but an unfiltered, emotional sort of thankfulness that is full of pain and full of joy. And yes, those two things can happen in one's heart simultaneously. I feel this thankfulness to my core. Each moment I am in, I get to keep. I'm not so sure about the next one. So, here now, for this now, thank you Lord.

These moments are precious, friends. The small moments... they are the ones that become really big moments. Don't miss them. Don't let them slip by.

Thanks for listening...

Bekah

NOTES

PART THREE

A DIFFERENT KIND OF BEAUTY

BLOG ENTRY: AUGUST 2015

These days have been hard. They stretch me to new limits, expanding my soul and eyes to new things—mostly painful things. It's always weird for me to answer the question, "How is Titus doing?" My response is always along the lines of, "Um... well, he's good? I guess..." (Awkward silence.) I mean, really, what do you say to that? "Well, he's dying, but you know... We're good!"

Last night, I dazed off until my husband interrupted and asked what I was thinking. I told him he didn't want to know. It wasn't very uplifting. When he pushed for the answer, I declared I wanted our normal life back, the one where two rambunctious boys drove me absolutely crazy, ran me ragged from sun up to sun down. But it's gone... I can't get back there.

I live in two worlds right now. The one where I'm grasping for any thread of control over this situation—just one ounce of human promise that I can step in and save my sons from this monster that is Batten Disease. In this world, where we feel control is necessary for survival, it is easy to understand my grasping for it. Of course I feel this way and seek control!

But the second world I live in is this obscure world of joy. Joy. I don't use this word lightly. What does it even mean to have joy in the midst of this heartbreaking place, where we've been cheated of all we thought we should experience?

And, honestly, in the midst of such loss, what business did I have feeling the light yoke of Christ? How dare I experience happiness or freedom. How dare I "joy"!

I should be consumed with anger, sorrow, fear. Surely those emotions will get us somewhere. Anger can become a call to action!

But here's the thing. I've found that joy means being fully present in a moment, fully feeling the pain we are in, and still finding the courage to claim thankfulness. Finding the ugly-beautiful.

Fully feeling pain lends itself to fully feeling joy. I do feel anger, sadness, and fear, but I also feel joy!

What God has given me rises above circumstances. My joy is purely based on the beauty of who God is, not the ugliness that has come upon our family. My joy is based on a God who is good and loving; who feels this pain with me. Who is in control, with our best interests in His heart. This doesn't change. It won't change if a cure is found to save our boys. It won't change if this disease takes them away from us.

So now I know, I can have joy even in this. And when I see lives changed, when I see people learning of deep, secure, safe love in Christ because of our story, I have joy. It's a major perspective shift and—how dare I say what I'm about to say. Should I? Okay, well, here goes...

What if this disease that looks so ugly through our worldly eyes would look different if we put on our Jesus eyes? Think about it. We see the path Jesus took to the cross, being crucified—an intense, horrific, painful death—and we call that path good! GOOD! Really? How could we ever call that good?

Well, we know the end of the story. We know that it had to happen that way for sin and death to be conquered. To loosen the grip of death around us. When Jesus came back from the dead, proving He could overcome all (yes, even death) and make all things good (yes, even crucifixion) then why can't our situation be seen as good?

Because I know the end of the story here, too. I don't know exactly how it will play out, but I know Titus and Ely's story will reach people who would otherwise not hear about God's deep, intense love for them. I know Titus is being loved even now in ways I can't imagine as his spirit remains, but his body fades. God is with him. I know that someday, Titus and Ely will be wrapped in the arms of the One who loves them most: Jesus. They will no longer be bound to this world in horrible ways, but will be free!

Could we ever grasp this understanding of His depth of love and goodness if our days were always sunshine and smiles?

So yes, how dare I "joy." How dare I find new breath in this situation.

Having joy in this life does not numb me to the pain of it. I can't tell you how many times I've cried... like hard, ugly cries. How many times I've pleaded with God to change the storyline. How many times I've felt such deep pain when a picture pops up or a video is watched and I see the Titus I know is still inside.

I believe Jesus felt every ounce of pain on that cross, as much as anyone else who was ever put to death in that dreadful way. And pain, yes, I feel it. To the core. And almost more so because I've opened myself up to fully feel joy, to seek the God moments and good in our situation. This keeps me going. It keeps me from numbing over, from checking out to protect my heart. Because I seek to feel joy wholeheartedly, it means I also feel pain wholeheartedly. I feel helplessness, lack of control, emptiness... And that's okay.

I leave you with a quote by Ann Voskamp.

In her book One Thousand Gifts, she explores if our dark pain could actually be the genesis of new life.

"Yes. And emptiness itself can birth the fullness of grace because in the emptiness we have the opportunity to turn to God, the only begetter of grace, and find all the fullness of joy."[2]

Here's to a new, full, joyful life.

Thanks for listening...

Bekah

CHAPTER EIGHT

A NEW PARTNERSHIP

I sat on the couch across from my therapist and tried to find the words to explain the difficulty of marrying joy and pain. It all seemed foreign and awkward. I felt like maybe I couldn't feel one if the other was present, but somehow it was denying a level of authenticity my soul craved and knew needed to exist. How could I be true to the brokenness of my heart while still honoring the truth in my soul that my God is victorious, even as I felt this pain?

She guided me through an exercise. My left side was pain, my right was joy. I was to sink into joy on my right side, and when it felt right, tap briefly in to my left side—pain. As soon as I would feel the emotion of pain in whatever scenario I was thinking of, she instructed me to move back to joy. I moved through several back-and-forths, tapping into memories that felt whole and right and redeemed, and then journeying to the deep dark places of bitterness, regret, and desperation. Then back again to the other. Over and over, as I visited each side with intentionality, I found a middle. I didn't expect it. I thought the two were like winter and summer. They couldn't exist together. But there in my back-and-forth journey I found a place where they merge. And not just merge, but tell the story of the other, almost exactly as fall tells the departing of summer and the coming of winter. As I reflected on pain, joy was illuminated. And as I reflected on joy, the same was done with my pain. Each told the story of the other in a way that opened up a depth to pain and joy I would never have known if I hadn't looked at them together.

To grasp the depths Christ went for me is to grasp the level of brokenness He experienced for me. To conquer death took facing death, experiencing death, and inviting death in to end it once and for all.

As I experienced this loss of my son and his "normal" life, I dove into the experience of death affecting us in a very close, personal way. In the midst of this experience, watching my son's earthly body fail him and knowing my other son was next, I was invited into a victory over this criminal called death even as it swallowed us whole. I knew we wouldn't be able to fight it. There was nothing we could do to pause the disease, to gain more time, to combat it. To know that the One who loves bigger and greater and sees all, has already combatted this evil and won—Oh, how I needed an invitation into the joy of that victory. And that's exactly how we survived day in and day out.

As my son grew sicker and his body weakened, we gained more equipment in the home. We gained suction machines, breathing treatments, chest vests that shook the junk in his lungs loose, and cough assist machines that helped him clear it all out. We gained oxygen masks and tubes and concentrators. We gained a hospital bed and feeding tubes. We gained more and more medication and dosing times throughout the day. We gained oxygen odometers, constant temperature readings, massaging of muscles, and stretching exercises for limbs that were losing range of motion. We gained diapers and large pads to lay under our son so messy diapers wouldn't ruin the furniture. We gained specialist after specialist, day nurses, night nurses, therapists, hospice, social workers. We gained middle-of-the-night scares that prompted us to ring that on-call hospice number multiple times.

We gained hospital visits, vomiting, bladder infections, and learning how to catheterize our son so he could urinate. We gained kidney failure and dementia. We gained silence from our son as he could no longer respond to us. We had to become good at guessing if we were doing the right thing and making accurate decisions and choices. We gained insanely long vocabulary words to describe diagnoses, medications, and medical conditions. This list of gains was exhaustively long. And this was the normal our lives had become.

Our lives moved to the rhythm of whatever Titus needed as we watched over him 24/7. Our fun dwindled down to friends making house calls and turning on our favorite movies so Titus could hear something instead of sitting blind in the quiet.

Not what I expected my parenting journey to look like.

And yet, each day, I began to recognize other gains. Because in light of all the painful gains, illuminating bright in our unblinded eyes were these joyful gains, too!

As my son grew sicker and his body weakened, we gained friendships and support. We gained home-cooked meals and friends willing to sit in the quiet and just be. We gained help with house cleaning. We gained willing hands to care for our boys so Danny and I could cherish and protect our marriage, as were given the gift of time and rest together. We gained redemption as we shared Titus smiling while we stomped his feet like a dinosaur and heard how he inspired others to keep taking that next stomp in their own struggles. We watched God work through our story, reaching the deepest of hurting hearts and that was a gain we felt in our souls. We gained donations of all kinds to provide all we could hope to provide for our boys, given in the most beautiful, kind, and generous of ways.

I must pause here to tell a story of that generosity we experienced as a family. As we neared Christmas of 2015, my desire was for all our family to be together.

Our church began asking us, "What needs to be done?"

And we answered.

Finance troubles stood in the way for some of our family members to get to California. A church across the country heard about this and raised money and airline points to ensure everyone could be there.

A generous individual from our previous church in Illinois wrote a check that payed for a vacation home rental just down the street from our house so everyone could stay free of charge.

Our home church in California organized a meal train and provided three meals a day for our family for 10 days! They took on the entire load of meal-prep so we could enjoy our company.

Our church also opened its doors for us on Christmas day so we could enjoy a larger space for dinner and gift giving. They had it beautifully decorated for our special time together.

Our boy's therapy team put on a night to remember out on the Newport Beach harbor for our family and friends to gather together and enjoy the Christmas lights.

It was an incredible Christmas. One I will always remember and has been imprinted deeply in me. And it was a pivotal moment of change for our faith community. Our pride could've gotten in the way, but we needed our people, so we said yes. They also needed us to say yes. Because we allowed them into our lives in the midst of a vulnerable time, we invited them into our story and in turn, we linked together into a greater story—God's. What a gain!

Perhaps most importantly, we gained a new perspective and clearer vision. We stopped trying to run from pain and avoid its presence. Our blinders fell off. We stopped looking for ways to preserve what was in our buckets, which only led to temporary fulfillment. Rather, each moment gifted to us filled us to overflowing, and in that overflowing we watched the grace of God work miracles in our hearts. We poured our buckets out in an offering to Him. We knew our pain wasn't all there was to this life. But acknowledging it allowed us to see that there was so much beauty to behold in the deep-down darkness.

It was as if I was on the front row witnessing the most epic rescue of all time. I felt I was given the inside scoop. I was in on the secret. That victory was coming and was indeed already ours. And, psst... don't tell the enemy, but guess what? *You and I get to live victorious, even now.*

BLOG ENTRY: OCTOBER 2015

I'm sitting here wide awake at 2:30 am. It's frustrating because sleep has been evading my son for a while now and just when he finds it, I lose it. I've been on the verge of panic mode; that's why I can't sleep in these wee hours of the morning. Usually I can shove the fears out of my mind and replace them with truths, but right now they haunt me. And I realize I need to take them on. To allow each one a platform so I might be able to deal with them individually. I need to deliver a prison sentence that lasts instead of turning around to find that my fears have retrieved a 'get out of jail' card and are wreaking havoc on my life.

The truth is, I'm afraid.

I'm afraid I don't have what it takes to do this. What happens if this is true? What if I crumble leaving nothing left but an empty shell? What if, despite all my efforts to evade depression and grief, sorrow and heartache take over and they are all I'll ever feel again?

What if the only thing I will have left is you, God? All else is gone. My whole identity of who I am in this life, my dreams, my everything.

Because there are days it feels entirely possible.

I keep mulling all that over. I'm terrified by it, to be honest. That road feels too painful. I cry that classic ugly cry. I beg for You to change things. I can't do this. I can't give You everything and allow You to take away if that's what You choose. I can't.

How would I live in such an empty shell of life? No breath, no sustenance, no control.

But wait...
There is still YOU, God.

And in that moment, all I will see is You. Nothing else to filter You through, nothing to hold as leverage, nothing to put blame on or put my faith in. It is only You.

And because I believe You love me and have great plans for this pain my family endures, I know in my heart I wouldn't just be surviving. I'd be thriving. A flood lamp beaming deep into my soul, through every part of me, only You. Your goodness, your love, your peace, your "fully enough."

I find myself reminded once again how small I am. When I grasp this concept, I live and breathe in the fullness of God. If I try to live in the means of my physical body, my control, I will surely suffocate and succumb to despair. But if I can live within the means of His Spirit working in mine, my very lungs expand when all around me says they should be constricting. I'm pulling new breath in places I shouldn't be breathing at all.

It occurs to me that this might sound heartless. How can I so easily write off all that fills my life now and accept that even if all is taken, I could still be full?

It's not an easy write-off at all. My heart has been filled with so much love because of my boys, my husband, my family and friends. And that love source comes from God. He doesn't just have love... He IS love!

I have two choices. First, I could choose to grasp tightly to my worries, my fear, and my need for control, which is really putting two hands around my throat and squeezing tight...

Or...

I can accept this incredible gift of love God has poured on me. And when the day comes in my life when all that's left is Him, I will still have love. I know the same promise of love is extended to my family. I could never provide that kind of everlasting, thirst quenching, joyful kind of love to them out of my own means. It is of Him. So, despite the pain of our circumstances, I find myself waiting in anticipation. What is God going to do?

Anticipation is a funny thing. It can be exciting or it can bring on anxiety! I just learned a new term: anticipatory grief. It's a term that attempts to define a complicated combination of emotions. For those of us caring for terminally ill loved ones, we grieve daily over what has been lost while simultaneously trying to live in the moment, enjoying the now, taking in whatever we can before all is gone. It can become quite the merry-go-round. I need a firm foundation in the midst of the crazy cycle. I hold tight the anticipation of what God will do.

He doesn't expect us to live these lives full of difficulty with no promise of redemption. Rather, He uses all things for good, redeems it all! What anticipation I have of what God is going to do through our story, through our sufferings.

So, I come back around to my fear—the one of losing everything. I'm reminded that we won't lose at all. In fact, we will gain! The day Titus leaves this physical world, he will be in the arms of Jesus! I imagine Jesus meeting him with a big, black, shiny train engine and letting him drive it and pull the horn. I can see my son, able to run, dance, talk, shout with joy! I love to imagine my Gramps and my sweet Grandma Naomi there to greet him, perhaps getting in on the train ride themselves. Oh, the anticipation I have for what God will do.

I imagine embarking on a journey to fight Batten Disease and, along with many other amazing families, joining the fight to find a treatment or cure. Could God use us in this way?

Oh, the anticipation I have for what God will do.

I imagine lives that feel dark and lost, stumbling upon our story and seeing truth shine through and love broken free. Perhaps they would see just how loved and treasured they are by our God. Oh, the anticipation I have of what God will do.

I wouldn't have written our story this way. But I'm here to say again, "Yes, Lord. I will go..." Wherever there is. As fear rises and my perceived control slips away, my throat constricts and tears run hot, may I be reminded that I will always have You, God. And I can wait in great anticipation for the wonderful, good things You will do.

Thanks for listening...

Bekah

NOTES

CHAPTER NINE

EXPECTANT ANTICIPATION

I have always been a sucker for a really good story. I love complex characters where good and evil are sometimes a bit hazy. It feeds something in me when a writer helps me empathize or even like the bad guy. Real life is that complex. None of us are entirely good or entirely bad. We have glimpses of both, even if we strive to be good most of the time. But when a story can take me through the eyes of a character into her world where I feel, empathize and lose sleep over her life obstacles, I give it two-thumbs up. It is as if I can work out some of my own struggles, imperfections, and worries through this character in a safe space. My life gets put to the side, but the hard work of life is still getting done as I live in the fictive bubble.

There is another good book in which the same can be done, yet it does not contain a fictive bubble. In fact, it is the first story, the longest story, and the last story that will ever be told. The Big God Story, held inside the Bible, and still continuing to this day as you and I are living in it, is the greatest story ever told. I fell in love with this Big God Story at a young age in Sunday School, but then the stories grew familiar, repetitive, and old. The ending was so predictable! God wins! Who knew?

It wasn't until I became a children's pastor that I fell in love with the stories of the Bible all over again. I dove into the interconnectedness of the entire storyline and taught my kids the same. It was magical. We were all connected to this story! There were characters who struggled to do the right thing, had moments of heroism, got defeated, wished for death, led entire tribes to freedom, got sucked into temptation, witnessed miracles, performed miracles themselves, established the first church, and so many other things.

As I dove in again and again, I realized this was my heritage. How incredible to have this story as a predecessor to my very own story! I took on real life as I read about these characters. It was invigorating.

But then a final form of evil came knocking on our door: Death. And I couldn't deal with it in my own power- my own kind of brave.

All those Sundays of teaching hundreds of kids about the power of God, the trustworthiness of God, the faithfulness of God, the redemption of God; I had to go back and decide—did I really believe in *that* God? And if I did, what does *that* God look like in *this* story?

My favorite Bible story of all time is Joseph. Although my storyline is different from his, I find myself able to identify with him. I'd like to think it's because I'm the favorite child of my parents, but I think my baby princess—I mean, *sister*—might have me beat.

But really, Joseph seems to be a dependable, good guy. I can identify with that. As I watch Joseph, who is generally a good guy, in spite of the fact he does think a bit much of himself, get sold in to slavery—I find myself sucked in. God can't let something like that happen to Joseph!

It gets worse. For starters, he was sold into slavery by his brothers, who then faked his death and took his coat back to their father dipped in goat's blood, telling their dad that he'd never see his son again! Boy, my ability to identify with Jacob, Joseph's dad, sunk right into my soul as I was living in a current reality of death sneaking in at any time to take my own son away.

As Joseph maintained his integrity and looked to the One who could care for him in a land of enemies, he began to get noticed. The country's leadership called upon him to oversee Pharaoh's household.

Pharaoh's wife really liked Joseph too, but when Joseph refused to give in to her lustful demands, she cried wolf, got him in trouble, and sent him to jail. Joseph spent years in jail serving those around him and using the gifts God gave him while in there.

Years later, Pharaoh needed a dream interpreter and none of his dudes were doing the job accurately. An ex-convict who found himself employed yet again by Pharaoh said, "Hey, wait a minute, there's this guy I met while I was in jail. He interpreted my dream and it actually came true! You should ask him what your dream means." Joseph was released from prison and interpreted the dreams Pharaoh had been agonizing over. His interpretations were correct. Joseph was promoted to second in command over the country. Not only did he get promoted to a place of dignity, but he was moved into a position where God would use him as a rescuer.

As the years passed, famine struck. There was no food where Joseph's family lived, yet God had given Joseph wisdom in Egypt to save food from previous years. Joseph's family made the journey to Egypt in search of food. To their relief, they found food. To their surprise, they found Joseph. Through the power of forgiveness, Joseph was reunited with his father and brothers, able to save his people, and through him,

God preserved the blood line of Christ.[3]

There is a series of books titled, *That's Good! That's Bad!* by Margery Cuyler. I love the ride her books take us on. Her hilarious scenarios and characters' antics take you on a ride you are convinced is good until it all goes south. And then, when all hope seems to be lost, it takes an unexpected plot twist landing back on greener pastures. But just when you thought the livin' was easy, no-good-very-bad-days were right around the corner. That's exactly what I think of when I read Joseph's story. And suddenly, now, I find myself identifying with it, too.

Seizures—Oh, that's bad!

Prayer warriors surrounding us—Oh, that's good!

Making a big move away from our entire support system right in the middle of heavy medical scares—Oh, that's bad!

Moving to our new community to find the exact right doctors who would help us find answers—Oh, that's good!

Batten Disease diagnosis—Oh, that's really, really bad.

Learning how to live in every moment with love at the forefront—Oh, that is so very good.

Watching a disease take my son's ability to speak or see—Oh, that's more than bad. It tears at my soul.

Learning that one can indeed live life to the fullest even blind and mute and unable to move because Christ is in us and never leaves us and communes with us—Oh, my heart needed to understand this. It is so very good.

All throughout this journey, I have learned and continue to learn that what I see before me will never be the whole picture. May the term "It is what it is" die a quick death. It never is what it is. God is always at work weaving together what we could not even imagine. And it is so very good. He spins on its head what looks to be ugly, painful, and bad. In turn, it becomes beautiful, perseverance-building, and redemptive.

And yes, good.

This is the radical perspective shift that has happened in me. In the heat of these terribly bad Batten moments, the pain is great. But knowing and experiencing His grace and provision all throughout the bad makes me aware that there is something amazing happening even in the hard moments. I learned that when things get hard, it's generally not wise or beneficial to run away. It's better to push through, but not on my own strength. I don't have the foresight to weave good through all of this. But He does. And He invites us in to His story.

We get to be part of this Big God Story. Wow! I know God is up to something big. I know I get to be invited in to take part in it. And I will say yes over and over and over again.

I sat upright in bed; my body drenched in sweat. In my semi-conscious and confused state, I had to take a moment to decipher what was reality and what wasn't.

Reality: My husband and both boys were tucked safely in their beds.

Reality: All was well. Time to go back to sleep.

Not Reality: I'd had, yet again, a nightmare about losing track of my boys when they were around a large body of water. And my nightmare always ended with me desperately trying to save one or both of my boys as they fearlessly succumbed to the deep waters. It swallowed them whole.

I repeated the nightmare. Night after night after night. We were still fairly new to California. Living near pools and the beach was a new thing for me. Playing in the water with my two young boys was a new thing for me.

During the day, our playtime in the water was some of the best family fun! But fear always ate at me. Don't let go! Don't take your eyes off them. They could die under your watch and you are here to protect them!

The nightmares slowed down as winter came, when the air cooled just enough to make trips to the water less appealing and we moved on to other activities. But for months, that nightmare haunted my sleep, telling me that I couldn't protect my kids enough, that no matter how alert I was in my dream, it was strangled out by a nightmare as my sons were drawn to dangerous waters and swallowed up again. Over and over.

Danny noticed. I was restless and tired during the day. I continually asked myself, why this intense fear of losing my boys and not being able to protect them? In these nightmares, my voice never worked, my legs always moved too slowly. I couldn't save them. All was out of my grasp, my control. And it devastated me night after night, week after week.

Also a reality: Both of my boys have a genetic neuro-degenerative disease that cannot be cured or, at this point, stopped.

Reality: I cannot save my boys and they are dying. It is a nightmare brought to life. Fear that disables. Depression that overcomes. Security uncovered as an illusion.

This disease has ravaged Titus's body quicker than we could've seen it coming. How did I miss it—the last time I'd hear him roar or see him tackle his brother? How do I live courageously, still the mama, the protector? But with no control?

Fear seizes. Fear cripples. Fear blinds.

Fear kills.

It kills beautiful moments. It kills the ability to see those moments when blinded by harsh reality. It kills moments of closeness in relationships. I can't be here, fear. Take my place setting away. I'm leaving.

I can't sit in a complacent tolerance of auto-piloting to fear. Yes, it's the easy response. But it's the cowardly response. And it's not of God.

Today I will protect my boys by knowing full well who my strength lies in; who my trust lies in. I will not return to fear today. I will look to Him, the one who knows exactly where this is all headed and promises goodness. I will walk this path with Him no matter how brutal the world feels. Because today, love and joy get to win. Today we get to find beauty, not fear, in Him.

Thanks for listening...

Bekah

NOTES

CHAPTER TEN

CRIPPLING FEAR

People often explain grief like giant waves. That's how fear was for me. A wave of fear would crash down, my whole being caught up in the wake of it, unable to run away in time.

I was walking the aisles at Target one day looking for some new clothes for my ever-growing boys. I could still shop for Ely in the toddler section, but Titus had grown long enough that he needed the big boy section. As I searched through the racks for size 6 slims, my eyes scanned across the sizes: 8, 10, 12.

My breathing accelerated and my heart began to race. I looked around to see if anyone had noticed the storm brewing underneath my surface. I blinked back sudden tears forming like an army that had just laid siege on my wall and were climbing their way up to attack.

"You are going to lose your son," the little fear army taunted.

"You'll never get to buy these sizes for your son."

"You are going to lose so big you'll stop functioning. Nothing will be left. You won't even be able to look at these sections anymore."

"Look at you, coming undone. What a mess."

On and on and on, this narrative spun in and out of my brain synapses, fear acting as the carrier. Before me on that clothing rack was a future I wouldn't behold with my son, unless God chose to intervene with a miraculous physical healing. And in that moment, nothing scared me more than a future of separation from my son. My breathing became so ragged, I knew I needed to get to the car. I escaped the store, dropped to my seat in the car, and lost it. I cried out. I begged. I pounded the steering wheel. I screamed at Batten Disease. This disease was going to take us all down.

My mind wandered to the conversation we had days before with our hospice team. We were asked to consider whether we wished to fill out a do-not-resuscitate form. They wanted us to think through what our wishes would be in the end-of-life stage for our son. It all felt completely unthinkable.

No, not just unthinkable—ferociously unfair!

I felt my fear turn to rage over big boy clothes and medical forms, and then to bitterness. I thought of my family and friends who got to experience life seemingly untouched by pain. They took their kids to sports practices and games. They did homework at night and had difficult conversations with them. They recorded cute sayings and expressions and watched their children's personalities grow from little people to big. They got to invest spiritually in the growth of their children, speaking the identity of Christ into them as it captured the hearts of their children and took root! I knew that typical parenting came with challenges. In that moment, I wanted those challenges. I wanted the "F" on the report card and the child coming home bullied, because it would mean I would still be holding my child.

"Now hold up..." a Voice whispered. *"Child, begin to speak truth to yourself."* It was a gentle reprimand, for nothing really is what it is. There is always something more at work. The roots of my heart that have woven around my Jesus, clinging to Him for nutrients, began to pulse with life and air.

I took a deep breath, and I spoke out loud.

"You God, are victorious even over this."

"You have defeated all brokenness. Even death."

"My life is Yours, and even if I lose, it's still Yours."

"You are in me and I am in You. There is nothing I could accomplish or add that would make me more Yours than I already am. Nor is there anything I could do that could make me less loved by You."

"All of this life is a glorious sandcastle—chances to see You build Your grace, Your hope, Your love, and Your abundance in all things, always. My sandcastles will fall and rise, but You remain constant in it all."

"My inability to always understand, comfort, and guide my son leaves me feeling so inferior and ill-equipped, but you, Lord, hold him in ways I cannot. You speak to his very soul and comfort him beyond the ways of this world. He is Yours and Your love runs so deep in him that he experiences your victory even in a body wretched with Batten Disease."

I breathed out, shaky in that afternoon encounter. An important reminder clearly reinstated in my heart: truth must always be present. Truth was a weapon. But not a truth of harsh words; rather, words that soothe the soul and remind the heart of a message of courage. A courage-filled message that says, "Move over fear, you don't get to drive."

BLOG ENTRY: FEBRUARY 2016

To be completely honest, it's been hard as new things pop up in my mind, plans we will need to consider for Titus. And, as much as I'd love to say I'm always kind and loving, my selfishness and defensiveness have gotten the best of me. It hurts to let my guard down when it means I might not ever get it back up. Ever get to that moment where your brain just goes on overload and then quits working all together? That's where I'm at emotionally and spiritually. And then yesterday morning, God met me, like He does, as I sat to listen, knowing full well my ears were plugged and I doubted I'd hear a thing. Instead of speaking to me through my ears, He spoke straight to my heart.

I know what truth is. It runs through my head and even overflows to my heart. But I question my steadfastness in it. Does truth flee as soon as my anger flares? As soon as my physical needs aren't met? When I haven't had enough sleep? When I feel betrayed by a friend? In these moments, my fears come alive!

I open up to Matthew chapter 3 - the temptation of Jesus. He was alone, hungry - like 40 days and 40 nights fasting kind of hungry. He is in the beginning of His ministry. Along comes Satan tempting Him in vulnerable places. I've read this passage of scripture so many times. I am always in awe of Jesus and His ability to say just the right thing back. As I read the story again, God allowed me to see something new. Truth. The steadfastness of Jesus' replies—He zoned in on the lies so fast and answered back with resounding truth.[4]

I have so many days of being worn down. It might be the result of a sleepless night, too many doctors' appointments in a week, not eating right, arguments with my husband. Or sometimes all I can say is I'm spiritually exhausted. I'm run down. Satan has been beating me down little by little. There are days when the truth minimizes and my selfishness maximizes. Truth becomes the unfocused background in my picture of life and rather than turning my lens to see truth clearest, I focus on self. I focus on my needs that aren't being met. And then I start getting angry. Over life, toward the disease, at all that has come upon our family. But rather than turn to God to be filled with truth, hope, and peace, I turn to my bitterness to be filled with depression, anger, and joy sucked away. The way I go about my day begins to feel lifeless. All I can muster the energy to do is watch the clock tick by. My God-given gifts are frozen in time, something locked away that I can't fathom accessing... too much energy, way too much. My boys get a shell of me. I drag my feet through the motions - detached because, well honestly, right now, to attach and feel takes more energy than I have and it's too hard. What has become of this joyful spirit in me?

"Where are you now, God?"

"WHERE ARE YOU NOW?"

I've yelled this so many times.

Always,

Always,

Always, my heart is wrapped in a quiet presence. I break. I've been standing "strong" for so long, but really that version of me is a hardened empty shell that symbolizes strength in the world's eyes, but not in my God's. My God is okay with emotion. My brokenness welcomes Him, it does not deny Him.

And His response to me?

"What do I ask you to put on each day, Daughter?" Of course. I turn quickly to a scripture that has impacted my life over and over again. Ephesians 6:10-18. The first part of that scripture?

"Put on the belt of truth..." I whisper. I feel the gentle reminder that I have forgotten to put mine on.

Truth: I am loved. Still. Always. Even in my ugly selfishness. Even in my drowning depression. Even when my smile doesn't meet my eyes. Even when I check out of life and check onto Facebook. Even when I say hurtful things to my husband simply out of my own insecurity. I am loved! I let that take root in me. When I remind myself that I am loved in those moments, lies cannot weave around my heart.

Truth: He is faithful! I can look back in my life, even to yesterday, and tell you how He provided exactly what I needed to get through. How He continues to do as He said. He has given me a new perspective, a heart that feels deeply for others, a love for my family that goes beyond love we are capable of on our own. He amplifies all that is good! I see my son do a silly dance in my own eyes and yes, it's funny and sweet and I love it. But when I see through His love in me, my joy in that moment is bigger, more satisfying. It's an amplified joy because I see God in it all. He reminds me that He is here. He never left. He is good. He is redemptive. These are all promises that He faithfully keeps.

Truth: This world is not all there is! We fight a very real physical battle against Batten Disease in our life. It's easy to focus on the disease, the constant care, the fact that my boys are not getting better. When I forget the truth that we are here temporarily, I get so caught up in the fear of death, of loss, convincing myself that if I'm not fighting for my child to survive in this world, I'm not surviving either. But what we experience here on this earth is not a temporary spiritual experience. It is a temporary physical experience because there is more! So much more for my Titus! For me! For you! And that is truth! Our reward for fighting the spiritual battle here is not death. It's the crown of life! Life with no pain, no sickness, no depression, no anxiety.

No Satan - you cannot have your way with me here. My son - he will gain when he leaves this world. That fear you are using to grip my heart even now, in this moment as I write, telling me I won't survive his loss, I won't have anything left, I'll be an empty shell... well, you've tried that already. And, as tears begin to fall again, I'm telling you to back off and get out, in Jesus' name! He has continued to prove that what you think ought to break me down, has in fact done the opposite.

"Dear brothers and sisters, when troubles comes your way, consider it an opportunity for great joy. For you know when your faith is tested, your endurance has a chance to grow. So let it grow, for when your endurance is fully developed, you will be perfect and complete, needing nothing." James 1:2-4 (NLT)

Truth: I am not living these hard days to survive in this world. What reward is there in that? There will always be hardships to struggle through, to survive. However, I live in this world to discover more about my Father, His love, and how to love others as a result. What life we have to gain!

When there is an absence of truth in my life, I'm at the mercy of whatever my circumstances and emotions feed me. There is no strong foundation to filter them through. I am up, I am down. I have no control - no, in fact - they control me. No more. Hold on to truth!

I am loved! He is faithful! There is more than this broken world! So, today, let my belt of truth glisten strong! Let my experiences today be seen through the truth of love, faithfulness, victory! I pray truth for your life as well, friends.

Thanks for listening,

Bekah

NOTES

CHAPTER ELEVEN

WEAPON OF TRUTH

've had many conversations with others about truth. What *is* truth, and what do we do with it? It appears that many days, we all may decide to live at the whim of whatever life throws at us. Our behavior, actions, and thoughts are tossed and turned according to the circumstances of life. I have felt often a bit like a meme with a blank face, caption reading: "Oh, is this what we are doing right now? Okay."

That is an accurate reflection of how I felt as we continued to tumble down the mountainside into the rare disease abyss. My motto had become, "A moment at a time." Yes, a moment. Even a day at a time was too much. At any given moment, we could find ourselves in a medical emergency or with a surprise gift of laughter, and we had to be prepared to embrace either one and go with it.

As we first began to travel this road, to say our lives were driven by circumstances would be an understatement. Our lives were hijacked by our circumstances and we were trapped in the mid-air flight, unable to fight free. Yes, my life felt entirely out of my control.

But control is not a substitute for truth. Truth can exist and ground us even in turbulent places that threaten to lift us off the ground and throw us this way or that way.

Truth became a faith tool that was essential to my survival. The inner self-dialogue that held lies I had always brushed off as harmless, weren't so harmless after all. In fact, without truth, they undermined my perspective and clarity, joy and hope. I needed truth to combat them!

That devastating diagnosis that told us we could not do anything for our son? I needed truth to combat it!

The emotions that followed us as circumstances ebbed and flowed? The happy and then the depressed, the overjoyed, the comfortable, the anxious, the angry? I needed truth to combat all them!

One of my game-changers during this time was reading Ann Voskamp's *One Thousand Gifts*. She challenged me to take off my blinders and choose to really see. I was spurred on to proclaim thankfulness and live in communion with Christ, both in the laundry folding and the tube feedings.

As I ran to appointments and held my boys close through the brutality of the disease, I experienced constant communion with Jesus. Truth rooted deep in me, creating a lens through which I experienced our circumstances differently.

As I practiced the spiritual discipline of proclaiming truth, I wrote myself a list I could go back to whenever I felt the battle of *truth vs lie* strike up again in my heart.

I titled it: *Ways to Settle Myself into Truth*

1. Start a gratitude journal. Write down one thing you

are thankful for each day. Make this a regular habit to revisit thankfulness and document it. When your mind is watching for things you are blessed with and blessed by, it has less time to be misdirected by circumstances. Thankfulness is the gateway to a perspective shift; giving eyes to see the good and beauty in the midst of drop-dead ugly places.

2. Arm yourself with truth. Our minds are like sand on a sea-shore. When circumstances come in with the tide, we are absorbed in them. When things get better and the tide goes out, we live in the comfort of the sun, but do nothing to protect ourselves the next time circumstances roll in. We ask God to rescue us, but we do nothing to set our mind on Christ. How do we become armed with truth? Through scripture, through God statements, through worship, through thankfulness.

3. Speaking of God-statements, write them all over your house. God-statements are truths that remind you of God's character, of His promises, of His faithfulness. Scribble them on the mirror in the bathroom. Put them on sticky notes up on the walls. Put them everywhere you really need to see them.
"He WILL redeem and has already redeemed!"
"He knows pain."
"He promises a hope that will not disappoint!"
"This *is* temporary. Victory is coming."

4. Find a safe place with a wise person of faith and speak the lies running through your isolated mind *out loud*. Often when lies live in our heads we have a way to make them sound smart, correct, and accurate. As soon as we begin to speak them out loud, we

realize how far-fetched, silly, and downright ugly these statements sound. We realize how mean they are. How filled with contempt they can be. And when we can speak these aloud to a trusted friend, they can help identify lies versus truth.

This scribbled list became a daily practice. The decorative mirror in my dining room had God-statements scrawled out across it. All over our home, I had written His Truth to remind me of whose I was and who my God *was* and *is* and *always will be.*

As I practiced discernment of truth, I found another ugly enemy who had built a home in my heart: discontentment. I wondered if I'd had this disease of discontentment for quite some time. Looking back through my life, I saw God's blessing over every step and new adventure we'd taken. I also saw how the timing of some of our new adventures had been so God-ordained. He had always given us exactly what we needed everywhere we'd lived.

But in the midst of those adventures, after the honeymoon had worn off, when we'd gotten down to the nitty-gritty, there was something in me that always felt unsettled, useless even. Maybe the glamor of the new job had worn off or my marriage turned out to be harder work than I thought it would be or a parenting stage drug me into the ring and took me through thirteen rounds of hardcore toddler takedowns. (Thirteen rounds... that's how many times I had to put Titus back into bed for his first nap in his big boy bed, guys. I think I cried. No—I know I cried. Oh, how I needed him to take that darn nap!)

At the first sign of conflict, I would begin to feel discontent. And the lie-filled dialogue told me, *I must not be where God had called me to be.*

A confession, if I may? I'm one of those weird people. I actually *like* change. I thrive in change. I find a thrill in what change can bring and stretch me into. But this attribute of mine can often dictate my life far too heavily. If things begin to feel stagnant, I look for ways to create change. As much as this is a God-given gift, Satan has found ways to twist it all up. In those moments of stagnation, I often began to play my discontentment reel; telling myself my purpose had run out and it was time to move on.

But truth held an honest mirror in front of me. What had discontentment done to my heart? Truthfully, it caused me to be bitter, snarky, flat, undevoted, apathetic, bored, jealous, angry, helpless, unimaginative, fearful. Yikes.

Allowing my feelings to be my north star served me poorly. For a time, contentment found in my circumstances and self-fulfillment made me feel good. But then that deep-seated tug for change always appeared. I found myself in that hopeless place time and time again, trying to fabricate contentment through my accomplishments, as something deep in me continued to go unfed, unheard, and unappreciated.

In one specific moment of bitter discontentment, where I felt all had been dictated for me and my creative energy and adventure were stolen, I asked God, "So what? You just want me to settle? To stick this out? To just be here?" As I asked, a little bit of my heart died because I had dreamed of more.

In that honest questioning, His truth came through in the words of 1 Timothy 1:6. God began, once again, to soothe my soul with His perspective that taught me there was so much more than what I could see.

"Godliness and contentment is itself great wealth." He reminded me.

What if the "more" I had craved was an adventure God was going to take me on in communion with Him? The adventure of contentment.

The truest sense of the word contentment does not rely on my circumstances. It isn't decided upon by the emotions of where I live and what I do and which titles I hold. No, rather, the purest form of contentment is based on the consistency and character of my Father.

As I found contentment in my Abba Father, I found perseverance to stay the course even when I had wanted to run away to something different. I found truth in my ache for contentment. That ache wasn't bad! Because as I searched for contentment in Jesus, I miraculously found new adventure, new breath, new perspective right there in the moments in front of me.

When I could bravely say adventurous contentment, found in my Father, happened in the middle of mundane tasks and sleepless nights—it was then I realized, the God of true contentment had put a new pair of lenses on my eyes. And oh, how I saw with new wide-eyed wonder the holy adventure that had surrounded us the entire time.

BLOG ENTRY: JUNE 2016

Before I dive in to where I find myself on this crazy, twisty-turny journey, I want to say something. I see you. I know you're out there. The one who had an unexpected loss, a heartbreaking diagnosis, the one whose life just got put into a blender and mixed around without a warning. I see you, now at the end of yourself not sure if you want to keep going. I see you as you fight for your marriage and at the same time wonder with every step if it's worth it; if it was really supposed to be this hard.

This is for you. For you who experience anxiety, the dark depths of depression, to those stuck in in the game of "waiting."

The truth is we are all broken. We all face uncertainty and heartbreak. This is a tribute to all that is hard, to all our unexpected plot twists. This hard life is so very real. May the storytelling of my life open up the opportunity to tell the story of your own brokenness, and through that, find a God of deep love.

I wanted to share my journal entry from this morning. It's an honest, vulnerable account of my heart:

I'm grappling with something. I feel unaligned. Or, maybe discontent? I can't explain it and I'm hoping by taking up the pen, God can work it out in me. I feel lazy, drained. And there are days I can't see past it. Like all motivation and energy have been sucked out of the house by a giant vacuum. My heart does not match my brain. I dream big. I want more. I want meaning. I want connection. I want creativity. I want difference-making. I want redemption. And I also want to be a mom to my boys in a normal setting. I want to hike and swim and zipline with them. I want to take them to sports practice and stand in the heat to watch a game. I want to document the crazy things they do and entertaining things they say. I want a marriage that is always at peace, where I always show love and kindness.

And yet, it's impossible for me to find a place where all these wants and my reality meet up. They don't cross paths. In fact, it's as if my wants are traveling in Europe while the reality is here in America. Completely different time zones, continents, languages. And so, disturbing discontent festers in my heart. And grief. Deep, deep grief.

We just got back from vacation. It was a good disruption to our daily routine, but it was hard! Would I have done it all over again knowing how difficult it was? Yes. But why can't, for once in our lives, something be all easy and all enjoyable? To experience something that comes relatively easy to most families, we have to work incredibly hard and sometimes, we have to fabricate fun. Make it be. We force our minds to think, "This will be fun, so believe it!" How badly I want to, but there are days I'm too exhausted.

The reality of what we face slapped me again a week and a half ago when I dropped my baby and hubby off at the airport to go see the Batten doctor in Columbus. Titus and I stayed home. He is so progressed the oxygen concentrator hums at all times now. My spunky, hyper, analytical, social, joyful little Titus has been taken away piece by piece by Batten Disease. I look at pictures of what was, and it feels like that boy is an entirely different person than the one sitting in front of me.

What's a mother to do? Well, I cry. That's what I do. I can't do anything else. I'm immobilized by pain and grief. All the "wants" versus "realities" are misaligned once again.

How did our story get written so wrong?

When did this unexpected plot twist happen and how can we get back there to rewrite it?

I grasp for this every night. Asking God to heal. To make it better. To make it right. And yet I feel the constant tug to let go. To continue to let go. I didn't realize how selflessly sacrificial parenting would require me to be. Every parent would tell you this journey of raising little humans demands selflessness. But this, to completely let go, release all my expectations, hopes, and a motherhood right to protect; this is a whole 'nother level and it's not one I signed up for. Yet, here I am—finding it a necessity to survive. It's not the letting go that gives me the survival strength, it's Who I am releasing these burdens to.

In every story I come across, I want to read through the pain, struggles, the hard. And I want to become so involved that when the hero wins, when the hero overcomes, it's beautiful! It brings happy tears and neatly folded corners where all the heartache our hero had to experience makes sense. All is redeemed and at peace.

I've been waiting for my neatly folded corners. Where are they? Why can't one day be met without struggle? Without my heartbreak pulling on the inside of me, threatening to spill out each night I put Titus to bed? Or each time I see a little boy his age run, or talk, or do normal 6-year-old boy things? Why can't I have one day where my stress isn't wound tight in my muscles, in my jaw; one day where tension isn't felt and my defensive coping strategy doesn't have to make an appearance?

It feels like too much to stay in this place where my heart is, but every pathway out is a slick uphill surface that I can't seem to climb up. There is so much pushing against me trying to create a reaction, or explosion rather, to the events around me. So much undefined. Too many what ifs. Heavy heartbreak. Rising in me like a volcano is this anxiety—a pressure to get everything in place exactly how it should be. To do everything perfectly so I don't mess up this opportunity I've been given to be a mom and a wife. I hit the pillow exhausted. And then it all haunts me in my dreams.

Where do I run? Because I want to run! Not physically away—I love my family far too much to desire that, but emotionally and mentally I want to run! I want to escape the premises to a secret garden where all is whole, healthy, and peaceful. Where there is a quiet that fills my soul and gives me new breath. Strength reaffirmed. Is there such a place without packing my gear and backpacking up an actual mountain peak? How do I control the crazy happening in my mind?

There is a life-giving, truth-building, love-rising, peace-perfecting, forgiveness-abounding place! It is in me! In the Spirit of God who takes up residence in me! And I want to run!

Run, daughter, run... full on to Me. Don't run to social media. Don't run to speculation. Don't run to pointless conversation. Don't run to coffee. Don't run to approval of others. Don't run to shopping. Don't run to your higher standards of what a mom should be. Don't run to your negative self-talk. Don't run to anxious what-ifs.

But, by all means daughter, do run...

To Me.

And I run. Because if I don't, I will get stuck. And once I'm stuck, it's hard to move. I run to Him in all my anger, anxiety, fears. I run to Him with all my gratitude, joy, and promises that I will be enough for this job of mom-hood because He is enough. I just run. Because what pulls me to Him is not just my brokenness, but His faithful promise to redeem!

I have no idea what the journey will look like as I run. I know full well that I'm running with a limp and my flesh screams at me to stop—it's too hard. But suddenly my lungs are filled back up, my mind is set forward, and I keep going. One moment at a time, one hour at a time, one day at a time.

And as I run, I begin to notice things. The welcomed breeze blowing through my hair. The breath that comes each time I draw it in. I hear birds chirping, leaves rustling. I'm here. He's here.

This heavy, heavy life. A life full of hurt, sickness, pain. I know exactly what I, in my flesh, ought to do... panic, worry, hate, protect, shut out. But I can't. That way is death. I've had enough of that. I need life.

As I stop to catch my breath, to take in a moment where He is breathing in and through me, I know that I can let God transform me into running to Him first. Into trusting Him first. Into a new person by helping me see a perspective full of truth, hope, love, and full life.

The truth is that maybe, right here in the midst of unexpected plot twists is where I, where you, need to be. Maybe this is exactly where God is going to meet us in the most real of ways. In our dirty, in our hard. In the very place where you feel your soul is being sucked out, He is going to fill it new again. Perhaps the "not-yet" or the "hard"- perhaps these soul-sucking places are where we will get the most soul-filling.

Thanks for listening...

Bekah

NOTES

CHAPTER TWELVE

EMBRACING THE UNEXPECTED

W e huddled together in the classroom, the one just off the foyer of our church home. The Elders of the church and our lead Pastor gathered around my husband, our boys, and me. In faithfulness and trust in the miraculous nature of our God, our Pastor laid his hands on Titus and Ely's heads and prayed for intervention. For healing. For the seizures to stop in Titus and the disease that had been planted in both their bodies since birth to be disrupted and done away with. I nodded. "Yes, Lord, please save my boys. Medicine cannot. Only you can."

Many were faithful to take Titus and Ely to the altar during their healing services. Our boys were prayed for in states all across the country and even in other parts of the world. Many boldly proclaimed his healing and were absolutely convinced God was going to heal.

But I struggled in my heart as I cared for Titus day in and day out with no improvement. While Ely remained asymptomatic (a fancy word for no symptoms), Titus's needs grew and his body continued to fail. I questioned my intentions, my faith. Maybe I didn't have enough faith.

Ah, lie! I searched my heart and knew without a doubt I was utterly dependent on my God; more than I ever had been. I was at my wits' end, and I knew I could not do this life on my own strength and power. I needed His.

As many continued to petition God on my sons' behalves, I began to ask God what He had for me in this, as their mom. In that asking, I felt the relentless tug to let go. But did that mean I was losing faith that He would heal my boys?

It was in this struggle, I learned of truth and hope found in the most miraculous of healings—a healing of the heart. This type of healing went beyond our physical world. It stretched across death and lived eternal. I remember a resolve coming over me in this realization: Titus and Ely didn't have to be physically healed to demonstrate God showing up.

This truth brought me to a place of great peace as I witnessed miraculous healings happening every day. In my heart, in our friends and family, and in complete strangers who heard our story. All across the country, hearts were being transformed and healed and drawn back to the God who had loved us all from the beginning of time.

Was God pulling us out of the dark and making life easy again? No, and I'm thankful He didn't, because it was in the deep darkness that we met with Him face to face. He touched my heart and allowed pain and joy to fuse together in such a way, I experienced both like I never had before. This was holy ground, this rocky, treacherous abyss I'd found myself falling into.

It was in this moment that I knew I would say yes to God no matter what the road ahead looked like. Because inside, I felt new and whole. My circumstances were the same, but my God was enough. My life was chaotic and exhausting, yet my heart found peace. I watched as an ugly disease stripped away my son, but my eyes saw beauty.

As I sat one day in Titus's room, looking at pictures from before we knew about Batten, the ever-present wave of grief flooded my heart. I closed my eyes, needing to meet my God in that moment. I needed Him in this storm. I knew when I looked out and only saw the storm, it was a sign to take blinders off; the blinders of fear, anxiety and bitterness.

I closed my eyes to the world around me and allowed Him to open me to His reality. The one where all of my unexpected plot twists were being worked for His glory and our goodness. And where a mighty Lord loved us so much, He gave us free will so we could decide whether we would love and follow Him, and in return didn't walk away when we walked away from Him. As our world spun out of control because of the brokenness and evil that runs rampant, He saw the brokenness and wove it together in a beautiful mosaic that would proclaim His love for us over and over again. What faithfulness!

As I closed my eyes diving into the reality of my God, I imagined my heart journeying on a broken path. Up above was a beautiful bridge, an easy trail to get from one point to the other. But our unexpected plot twist had thrown me off the bridge into the brush down below. It was in that dark, overgrown, rocky path that I learned again of a God who would go to brokenness for me.

It was subtle, but when I surrendered to the pain and surrendered to Him, a sort of kindling ignited inside. *This pain couldn't be for naught.*

I envisioned where I had fallen. I looked around to see a treacherous bridge ahead. It climbed large mountains and fell into deep ravines. It traveled beyond what I could ever know and see. And it was in that moment, I knew, I would walk this broken bridge. This brokenness was where I now lived.

And so, I familiarized myself with sorrow. As the life-raging waterfalls threw me to the bottom of myself, I looked up to see I had been washed up at the foot of the cross, and could see it at an angle I'd never seen before. He was utterly broken and beaten, given in to complete brokenness so that in our brokenness, He could become enough. The promise it held was glorious balm to my wounded soul. My grief, our loss, my not-enoughs, and what-ifs and if-onlys had brought me here.

I nodded in the truth that soaked through me. "Yes, Lord. You call me to a different kind of brave. It's not glamorous or easy. But in the midst of this broken place, You have revealed riches I could not treasure if I were on that perfect bridge. Up there, brave is temporary. What You have to share with me, this brokenly brave—it's eternal."

Am I foolish to still desire the uncracked, smoothly paved bridge far above me? I might be, for those walking above cannot see the beauty that lies deep in the dark cracks of my broken, overgrown path. And they don't yet know the victory to be had when one is willing to face brokenness.

NOTES

PART FOUR

LEARNING TO LIVE AGAIN

CHAPTER THIRTEEN

USHERING INTO ETERNITY

End of Life. What a phrase.

As the summer of 2016 came to a close, I felt in my heart that Titus's earthly life was also coming to a close. We had gone through so much with him and we plunged headfirst into it all. We embraced the role of parenting Titus, not just as mom and dad, but as a nurse, therapist, advocate, and everything else it took to care for an individual with such extenuating needs. I would have had it no other way. It was an honor to care for my son, and to have the resources and community help around me that made it possible. I will always treasure those moments.

But they were so hard. I cried as I laid next to him at night, listening to him struggle to breathe clearly. It made me sad every time he had to have blood drawn or take a medication that would sedate him. I hated having to put a tube down his nose into his throat to suction out the secretions he could no longer control and swallow on his own.

"How long does he have to suffer, Lord?" I would pray. And in the same breath, "Please don't let him die... please heal him." This was the paradox I lived in. The desperate prayer to allow him to live, the desperate prayer for God to take him so he would be whole and healthy and *Titus* again.

That late August brought many hard conversations with our hospice care team. The first was the acknowledgement that they, too, were seeing signs of the end of his life. I was handed a pink piece of paper and asked to consider marking our wishes about how much or how little intervention we wanted, should he stop breathing. To even consider not intervening if my baby stopped breathing made me sick. But I also knew, should Titus stop breathing, it would be his gateway to becoming whole, exactly as he was meant to be in the presence of Christ. How could I consider standing in the way of total healing? It felt there was no way to win.

Our team of care providers set up a time to meet together at our home. We invited our pastor and his wife, and my parents to join us. They were trusted voices to the conversation we would have.

Our hospice doctor, hospice nurse, chaplain, and social worker filed in and sat with us in a circle in our small living room. The doctor listened to Titus and checked him, nodding with solemn certainty. He sat down on the large bean bag chair we had in front of our window and began the conversation. I set my ears on his words, but when the message reached my brain, it took everything in me to stay present, the pain so deep my heart wanted to shut down.

The boy this doctor was talking about, the one who's lungs were filling up with fluid, whose kidneys and bladder were failing—this boy couldn't possibly have been running, climbing, and roaring around my home just 18 months ago. So much had changed. My heartbeat quickened and I began to panic. *No, this is too fast, Lord. I can't. I can't give him back to You yet. And just as quickly, Titus, I love you, and if this is what you are ready for, I will be there with you and hold the holy honor of ushering you into eternity to Jesus. But oh, God, this hurts!*

The doctor was speaking to us about signs our loved ones show us when they are ready. He spoke honestly about the deep confliction families have—whether to hold on or let go. He gave us permission to share our desires and wishes. I could hardly absorb that we were actually living in that moment, having that conversation in my living room about my six-year-old son. It was a surreal nightmare, and yet, supernatural peace rested over our home.

During a break in the conversation, Titus sleeping in my arms, I looked down and half-whispered, "Is this what you want, Buddy? Are you telling me it's time for us to let go?"

Those words came with a sledge hammer that, in one blow, shattered my heart. Because I knew it was time. I could see it in his exhausted body. His frame had grown frail, his organs were quitting. His breathing had become a struggle, and all he could do was sleep in drug-induced comfort.

My protective mama heart screamed out, *This is not the life my son deserves. I love him far too much to imprison him here in this failing body.* Every confession I spoke deep in my soul tore me up. He was still in my arms, still there with me. But for how long?

Our pastor spoke at the conclusion of the meeting. "Can we pray for Danny, Bekah, Titus, and Ely?"

I laid my son down on his pillow bed on the floor and we all stood, surrounding him in a circle, clasping hands, linking arms, all as one holding our brokenness up to the One who mattered most.

As we prayed over my son and over the days and weeks ahead, our pastor wasn't afraid to pray once more for a total physical healing. As our souls were being lifted to God through the unified prayer of our medical team and close supports, I imagined what our scene looked like from up above. What did God see that we could not, in that moment? My eyes were clouded with grief, but there was a buoyant peace keeping me afloat in the storm.

My son laid on the floor. I couldn't connect with him. He hardly woke up, and when he did, he was either blankly staring or crying in pain. I loved as big as I knew how and still fell short of what he needed. Fell short of rescuing him. Of reaching deep inside him and knowing all of his thoughts and fears and hopes and dreams. I felt so limited. But God. A reminder echoed inside my head. *But God knows. And He sees. And He holds. And He comforts. He loves, He gives peace. Oh yeah... and He redeems.* As my comrades lifted us in prayer, I saw a fully healed Titus lift up out of him and I knew in that moment, my son was held in a way I could never hold him. He was loved beyond my capability. He was redeemed, all of him made new by God, who was right there in the middle of our pain.

As we journeyed through the coming days and weeks, knowing we only had a few of those left, Titus's bladder started to fail. He was on more than 10 liters of continuous oxygen and his breathing sounded atrociously painful. He was hardly awake because we had to keep him sedated with strong pain medications. The liquid diet we were giving him was traveling to the wrong places and his lungs continued to fill up with fluid. It seemed as though the very last lifeline we had for him, his nutrition, was in fact hurting him more than helping. We tried to find the right balance, decreasing the volume until it was clear that his body could not handle nutrition of any kind. I couldn't wrap my mind around a decision to not feed my child. It was our last step of intervention that kept him here with us. After this, we had nothing left to tether him to this world.

I worked up the courage to contact a friend who had lost her child to Batten a couple years before. I had to know. Are we horrible to consider not intervening? To consider not feeding our child? To consider the fact that here, with us, may no longer be the best place for him?

Oh, the guilt that ravaged my soul. The lies that told me I was giving up on my son. That I didn't have enough faith to see him healed. That I just wanted this "inconvenience" to be done with so I could get on with my life.

Those lies...

They can tear you apart.

Lies, when stored away in the quiet, dark places of our souls, will grow and fester. My friend, who had gone through this before us, became my safe place to speak aloud every scary, unspeakable thought that went through my mind. I couldn't ignore this heavy decision. I couldn't sweep it away and pretend it wasn't occurring. There was no one who could step in and make these decisions for me and my husband.

As the lies and fears were spoken out loud, my friend reaffirmed us in love and truth. We found courage in the truth of our God whose love crossed bounds we couldn't even imagine crossing. God, who had modeled exactly what it looked like to put our child's best interest first, showing us that sometimes it means staring death in the face.

I was not equipped to handle this excruciating decision. The only chance of survival for any of us in that stare down was to remember who had truly won over this evil called death.

The truth was—*is*—that the God of love, of redemption, of sacrifice, of healing, has won. And this world—this broken, torn up and inside-out world—is not our eternal home. Our eternal home is with

God. We are passing through. This hard, temporary life can really dish it out, yeah? And if it hasn't yet, it probably will.

My heart breaks over and over and over again as I witness and experience firsthand, loss, heartache, broken spirits, and separation by death. It was never meant to be that way. But thank God, He sent Jesus to an ultimate stare down contest with death. One that became a sacrifice spoken over me that said, *"Even in this ugly, you are beautiful and you are worth it. Even if you hate me, I love you. I am always with you. You can feel me in the hugs of your loved ones. You can feel me in the community surrounding you. You can feel me in the heart-bursting love you have for your child. I am here and I am holding you. And... I am holding your child."*

As we stayed by Titus's side every moment of every day, I took great comfort knowing that Jesus was holding my son. He was holding him in ways I could not. He woke up two mornings in a row, squeezed my hands, and verbalized sounds. It had been weeks since I last heard his voice. What a gift! But ultimately, I could not connect with my son the way I desired to. And so, I poured my heart out to the One who could. The One who was preparing a beautiful place for Titus to come home to. There was peace. Always peace. I knew I was handing him off to much more capable hands. I knew that soon, my son would be running, somersaulting, laughing, and taking in the glory of God, just the way he should be. Perfect. I desperately wanted that for him. I wanted it more than I wanted to keep him with me in this state.

Our house had a steady flow of visitors coming to see Titus. Family flew in for their last goodbyes. Doctors and therapists who had cared for Titus throughout his years stopped in for a last hug and picture with him. Friends brought food in and stayed to pray, sing, and tell stories. We held vigil day after day, expecting the end to come at any moment. On Saturday evening, everyone decided to go home for the night, get some rest, and check back with us in the morning.

As I huddled down in the unusual quiet next to my son, I felt a strange prompting.

I whispered to him, "Go to Jesus, Titus. It's okay. Mommy will miss you so very much, but it's okay. I will live my days remembering your laugh and your hugs and your bright eyes. And I will see you again in Heaven. You don't have to fight to stay here because of me, or your daddy, or your brother. We want you to be healed. We all love you so much. So please, when you are ready, run to Jesus."

As I laid there next to him, his breathing sounded beautiful. It was clear and steady. Everything about him looked as though he was just taking a little nap. My husband, also by our side every step of the way, was observing the same thing. "Do you think he's trying to come back to us?" Danny asked.

My heart whirled in a free fall. If he's trying to come back, how could we push him away?

"I don't know. His body... it's not working anymore," I said. Tears starting pouring down my face. I felt myself growing frantic, hysteria pounding through my veins.

"Do we give him a little water or something?" Danny asked me.

I couldn't breathe. I couldn't speak. I couldn't hardly see past the flood coming out my eyes as I broke down, a wail escaping past my vocal cords. I didn't know. I didn't know what to do or how to make these decisions. Right from the get-go I was in over my head.

"I don't know what to do!" I bellowed out, moving away from both of them collapsing on the nearby ottoman, face in my hands, my whole body in panic-stricken sobs.

My husband reached over and grabbed me into a fierce hug. I could feel his agony. His deep desire to fix, to bring Titus back, but also his acceptance to let go even though it would tear him apart. "Bek, climb back in with Titus. He needs you next to him."

I did. I climbed back in and put both my arms around him, nestled him into me, kissed his forehead. His heart was beating so fast. I commented to Danny to come feel. Danny knelt beside us, his forehead against Titus', and whispered that he was there and loved him.

Together, we held our son in what would be our final minutes with him. At 10:52 PM on September 17, 2016, Titus took one last clear, beautiful breath, and then he was gone.

We had just been given the holy honor and terribly beautiful privilege of ushering him into Jesus's presence. Titus was home. My Titus was home. And in that moment, that was all that mattered to me. But my broken heart was not home. It was left behind. Even as deep peace remained, deep grief overcame.

BLOG ENTRY: NOVEMBER 2016

My beloved Titus,

I hope you are well. I miss you. And that is not a light-hearted sentiment... it is a soul-stirring, gut-wrenching "miss." Everything feels out of place now. You have gone away, and now a big piece of me has, too. I'm making it through the days, but many with tears just beneath the surface. So much of me is feeling incomplete, uneasy, always alert... like I'm in search of something that is missing because of the nagging feeling that I've lost something. Or someone. And I have... I've lost you.

I know, I know... not entirely. Your memory, your joy, your eternal life... those things are not lost. They are alive and well. I've had glimpses of you through others. One person shared that she had a vision of you playing with a lion, skipping across rocks in a river. You were having so much fun! You made your way back to your home where a feast was waiting for you and Jesus was your dinner guest. Hearing this from someone else made me so emotional. I took peace in it, but it was also weird. It's so unnatural to not be a part of your life now. To not know what you are up to. To not get the daily report from your teacher or brief paragraph of the day from your nurse. To not be by your side every moment, close enough to take care of every need as it comes up. To not be able to take in your laughter, your smiles, your bundle of energy. That was all so much a part of me, Titus. And it's all still so ingrained in me, but you are inaccessible.

This incompleteness in me makes me incredibly aware of my brokenness, and as a result, so aware of the brokenness around me. It's heavy. There is too much hate in this world, too much death, pain and sickness. And none of it is okay in my heart. All of it needs to be reconciled, but it feels too deep. Let's just be as honest as it gets... I am lost. I feel like a soldier returning home from war, attempting to make sense of civilian life under a new me. So, I stand here wondering, what's next? If I, if we, must live in this pit of brokenness, what is next for me, for your dad, for your brother, in that pit?

Titus, you made me smile so much. I still look at your photos all over our home and see old videos of you and I laugh and smile, feeling so much pride and joy! You are my son! And then it hits me that I can't turn around and see you standing or sitting behind me. And honestly, son, that still takes me aback. Because I truly can't believe that soul of yours, that crazy ball of energy, was snuffed out of life here on this Earth. It doesn't seem possible.

I left the house this morning because it was too quiet. Inside me the jagged edges of my heart were screaming for attention. I found myself beside a quiet bubbling stream, having a cup of coffee and writing this letter to you. It's not very eloquent, but it's all that is screaming inside coming out. It's my honest search for the rebuilding I hope and pray God will do in me as I stand lost and broken, knowing and trusting that in this pain lies His power and love and grace.

I'll end with this... a glimpse into the amazing memorial service held for you, son, just a few short weeks ago. These are the words God gave me to share in your service. I love you, son... And I'm so proud to be your mama.

The words I shared at Titus's memorial service:
"My baby has been gone for nearly six weeks now. I still hurt so bad. I miss him and have never felt so unable to fix and heal. My arms were meant to hold him, comfort him, love him, and now they are empty. The ache is worse than anything I've ever felt. I don't understand why. There is so much conflicting emotion in my soul.

The relief that Titus doesn't have to battle anymore.

The agony to not be able to hold him again.

The joy when I picture his huge smile and imagine his infectious laugh up in heaven.

The gaping wound in my heart that will be open for the rest of my time here on earth.

The anger that my child had to fight such a battle in the first place and had to face death at six years old.

The gratitude I have and pride I feel to have been his mom all those six years.

'Dance with Jesus, my sweet boy.' Those were my last words to him before they took him away.

I'm jealous. I would've loved to be right there with him, to see him transform and become whole again. To watch his ushering into eternity. When I think about Titus departing this world and starting life in heaven, I don't imagine my son waking up in front of a pearly gate with chubby baby angels flitting around. For some reason, I always imagine a huge train, operated by a Tyrannosaurus Rex engineer, pulling up beside him. The train is full, with my gramps, my grandma, perhaps other kids who fought a similar fight, all on board to welcome Titus. And as the train stops in front of Titus, the train conductor steps out. His eyes, His voice, everything about this man is familiar to my son because He has been with Titus through his valiant fight here on earth. And before the words 'All aboard!' can slip past Jesus's lips, Titus runs (yes, runs!) headlong toward Him. Perhaps, Jesus even cries happy tears as He sees my son restored to wholeness again—exactly as he was meant to be. Titus's face mirrors Jesus's own joy, his smile taking over his face, eyes sparkling alive and blue with a patch of brown on the left side. And just before he flings himself into Jesus's arms, Titus does a celebratory somersault, effortlessly rolls back up to his feet and jumps into the arms of Jesus. Titus and Jesus jump onto the train where big Titus-sized hugs are given out to the community of love surrounding him. The T-Rex takes them on a wild train ride, one that might resemble Roger Rabbit's ride in Toon Town and Titus's reaction exactly what you would expect, clapping, stomping his feet and cheering at the top of his lungs with a vibrant smile on his face.

I have learned so much through my son. A few years ago, I decided to start writing a letter to my boys. I thought I'd add on to it as the years went by, and when they graduated, they would have a letter of God's story at work through them. I thought these letters would be for my boys. Little did I know that through the letters I wrote to Titus, God would remind me of His redemption of all things broken.

In one letter, long before Batten entered our lives, I told Titus, 'Life hasn't been easy for you. But even through your struggles, you demonstrate pure joy! I keep using that word to describe you because I can't explain my little Titus any other way. You are joyful! Titus, I want you to remember this... the joy you demonstrate daily to us, is God in you. We don't have this joy out of nothingness. It comes from God and He is so good to give us this gift through the good and the bad.'

My next entry came after Titus started having seizures. We did not know what we were dealing with yet, but we knew his road was difficult. I shared, 'I want you to know, son, that even in the midst of your trials, you don't have to wait until you feel better or things are all going normal to shine or succeed. You've already proven to us that perseverance is totally worth it and we can't stop living life just because different issues come up. God is using your story to teach others about strength in Him and to open my eyes to the brokenness around us.'

The final entry I wrote to him followed our move from Illinois to California. It was a huge transition, getting all things medical, work, and school re-established. Once again, God was faithful. I needed Titus to know how much he was loved. 'Titus, you are SEEN by God! He loves you. You have never been lost on Him. We are nearing our one-year anniversary of your first seizure, and I am in awe of the way we have been carried through this time by God. God has created you to be amazing, Titus, and He will always be faithful to carry you through.' I was in awe then at the tribe that rose up around us, and I continue to be in awe.

The countless ways we've been loved by God through a tribe of a thousand others.... It's so humbling because... well, really, who are we to receive love of such magnitude? And it makes me wonder, why? Why are so many people joining us in this story? One of such pain and heartbreak?

God has shown me that Titus's story is about so much more than a little boy fighting a Batten disease battle. It's about all of us. Being invited into Titus's story invites us into something so much bigger than ourselves. It's being invited into brokenness. And oddly, everyone craves that because that's where we can be real. When we are willing to recognize that we are ALL broken, walls are torn down and the real work begins. This is the common ground on which all of humanity can meet. Brokenness under the shadow of Gods gracious wing can be life-changing, transformational. Healing.

Thank you, Lord, for this gift. Let us run toward this heartache and pain, opening it up for You to breathe into as we watch You redeem. Turn mourning into dancing, ugliness into beauty, and allow us to carry on the legacy Titus left behind of strength, perseverance, love, and joy only found in You."

Thanks for listening,

Bekah

NOTES

CHAPTER FOURTEEN

BROKEN AND FREE

I woke up. Somehow, I had managed to sleep a few short hours. When I came out of the room, my first instinct was to walk in to Titus's room and begin his routine. But his room was dreadfully hollow. The hospital bed, oxygen tanks, side tables on wheels, suction machines, syringes and tubes, monitors—all of it sat there without a patient to treat. No, that patient had been healed last night.

I walked dazed and disoriented to the kitchen. I noted that it was around 7 AM. My mental notebook said it was time to begin the morning medication routine and breathing treatments. My heart told my mind to shut up and stop talking about it.

But I couldn't stop. All the memories of the night before flooded in. The last breath. The wails. The urgent rush our loved ones made to our house after the phone call from Danny that Titus was gone. Our pastor and his wife, my mom, sister, and brother-in-law sitting together, holding Titus one last time. The stories. The laughter. The deep, gut-wrenching tears.

And then hospice came to confirm death.

And then the mortuary came to take my baby.

I remember laying him on that cold table with wheels outside our front door on the sidewalk. When they said it was time, I couldn't bear to see him covered with a sheet. I couldn't watch them load him in the back of a car as if he weren't just alive a few short hours before.

My next memory was the back of a head. It was our pastor. As I laid Titus on the metal cart on our sidewalk and released him into the care of strangers, I hit an emotional wall I could not climb. Pastor Steve ushered us back in through our front door, where his wife held me, my husband held in the arms of family, and we shut the front door. The back of our pastor's head blocked the view as he watched the team from the mortuary care tenderly for Titus. Steve became the guardian of our very broken things. He held the agony that was too deep for us to touch and became a bridge to get over the emotional wall on to the next moment.

And then I remember the goodbyes at 3 AM. My sister vomiting from grief as she tried to leave the house. My mom, Titus's Grandma, so broken and yet holding and comforting us in her arms. I saw Uncle Michael, who would be forever touched by his nephew. And a pastor and his wife who had pledged to take care of us a year prior to this broken night and had taken that pledge seriously.

I saw a husband who grappled between anger, sorrow, and relief that his son wasn't suffering anymore. He held me and I held him. Oh, that night... that gloriously holy, terrible, no-good, beautiful night.

I glanced at the clock and it struck me that I'd been standing in the kitchen for at least twenty minutes. Just standing. I felt so lost. My identity came crashing down around me. My entire life had revolved around Titus and his needs. Now he was gone, and so was my purpose.

At first, every 10:52 PM was pure grief-torture. My husband and I would watch the clock as it ticked closer and closer. We dreaded approaching *that* time. The one that would forever be tied to the time our son took his very last breath. Sleep would evade us, and each time 10:52 PM would approach, we would clasp hands and pray. That time held so much. It held deeply wounded goodbyes and hanging-by-a-string hopes. Our souls didn't know where else to go except the One who now held our son when we couldn't. And each 10:52 PM was a scarring reminder that we couldn't.

My mama arms ached so heavy for him. I remember the weight of holding all fifty pounds of him in my arms. He was so long and lanky, it appeared like I was trying to hold someone of my very same height. But that weight was nothing compared to the weight my empty arms now felt.

As the days passed by, 10:52 PM was less noticed, but every Saturday was heavy. As if passing each Saturday was a loud clock ticktocking its way further and further from the last time I saw my son's face. From the last time I created a memory with him. From the last time I felt his hand squeeze mine. It was a cruel ticktock.

Fear began to accompany me in my hyperawareness of times and clocks and tickings. *"You better not forget,"* It would sneer and mock. *"You won't honor him if you move on. You have no purpose now. Look at your empty, empty life. Oh look, it's Saturday. Remember that one Saturday you lost your son?"*

Weeks turned into months and the next marker to hold me hostage was the 17th of every month. Another ticktock away, another day, another month, and pretty soon, an entire year stolen from us.

During our last week with Titus, we had received an email from a doctor in Columbus, Ohio. She oversaw a clinical trial that involved enzyme replacement therapy for kids with Titus and Ely's disease. Ely was a prime candidate for their compassionate-use phase of the trial, which had just opened for enrollment.

That email came as I was literally counting Titus's breaths per minute. Pain and joy fused together in a way I had never experienced before. It was like the epitome of all we had been living the last two years, experiencing pain and joy simultaneously. There we were, saying goodbye to one son and beginning to hope for the other. As we spent every single moment of that last week with Titus, we had to prepare for Ely's future. They wanted to schedule his surgery for September 30.

I went on overload as my numb and empty brain organ tried to materialize a productive to-do list. We were to fly to Columbus on September 27. Just nine days away. All I could do was flee from pain. I escaped the house hoping for relief only to find it hurt just as much out in the world as it did inside my own door.

In the numbness, I sought out my Father. I knew my heart needed to bound back to safety through truth. I could no longer depend on my comfort zone to define what felt right and true. I was far beyond my comfort zone. I needed my Jesus to teach me exactly what this brokenness was really all about. Because if He didn't teach me through it, it would destroy me. I pleaded, I cried. Some days I took the next right step in front of me and other days I fell—a puddled mess before the King. I was at His mercy to squash under a grief-flowing sea of turmoil, doubt, and questioning.

We made it to Columbus to enroll Ely into the trial. We sent our baby, our only living son, into brain surgery, trusting his life with a complete, albeit capable, stranger. As he came out of the surgery as joyful as his brother, we watched Titus's redemptive story begin to play out before our very eyes. God's goodness-weave had never stopped wrapping around our hearts; we just had to be willing to put our Jesus-eyes on to see it.

We began a trek back and forth between California and Ohio for treatments every fourteen days. We lived ten days at home and four days in Ohio with a darling, spit-fire of a woman who we endearingly called "Bon Bon." Before ever having met, she heard our story through a mutual friend, and opened her home and her heart to us. In the months that followed, we didn't just travel to Ohio every other week for a treatment, we traveled to see Bonnie and all her friends. They became family.

The travel expenses were not covered by the trial. A man in our church got wind of our ordeal and set out to ride 1300 miles from Southern California up to Montana on his bike. In his Ride For Ely campaign, he raised awareness and enough funds for us to fly back and forth without financial worry.

In our bi-monthly travels back and forth across the country, I met many new faces in the various airports we journeyed through. Sometimes we'd wind up conversing with our seat companions, other times not so much. In those conversations, our story always came out.

"Where are you all headed?" a well-intentioned passenger would ask. I'd answer. And then another small talk probe, "Oh, you have family out there?"

I would observe my new seat buddy and determine what this poor unassuming individual could handle. Nine times out of ten, I answered truthfully. And so, our conversation would turn, "Rare, fatal disease."

I'd grunt. "Travel for experimental treatment. Yes, it's genetic. Oldest son just died from it." (It went something like that, but with a touch of "Bekah" as my husband refers to it. I promise, I don't actually speak in grunts.)

I always saw the struggle in their eyes as they searched for what to say next. Those conversation-starting questions are supposed to lead to small talk and I had just hijacked the conversation and laid it all bare. I heard a variety of responses. In most every scenario, I was blessed by these conversations, even though the other person often felt inadequate in their words. Honestly, I'd been through it and didn't have adequate words most of the time.

One particular response I heard often was, "I just don't understand why." And I wrestled with that.

Because, well, I know the answer.

But it's a monstrosity to tackle and it can become quite messy. But really, maybe we've got the why question in the wrong context all together.

A long time ago, in the beginning of this world, God created Adam and Eve. He gave them many incredible gifts, one of them being free will. God loved them deeply and created them in His image. He wanted them, in turn, to love Him deeply. He knew the only way that relationship could be returned authentically was if Adam and Eve chose by their own free will to love Him back. (Who wants to have to force people to love them in return?)

He did what any good and loving parent would do and He established boundaries that held Adam and Eve safe in His love. Satan, who had once been in the presence of God, turned against Him and infiltrated the beautiful garden where Adam and Eve lived. Satan used deception to lead them to believe they could be better, do better, achieve better than God was allowing them to be. All they needed to do was eat some fruit from the tree of good and evil and their eyes would be opened. And so, they ate.

Their eyes were opened...

And their hearts were shattered.

For God had been protecting them from the evil Satan wished to penetrate into them. What they had been protected from now ruled their hearts and minds. They felt things they'd never felt before: Shame, brokenness, incompleteness, fear. And so, yes, they could see good and evil like God could, but they lacked one distinct disadvantage...

They weren't God.

So began this complicated world where good and evil battle, and brokenness, sickness, pain, and sorrow run rampant. And death... Yes, death happens. This world wasn't supposed to hold death. It was created for life! For joy! For pleasure, for adventure, for community, for good! Not death.

When sin entered, death followed in and became certain. It touched my Titus. It touches everyone.

Everyone except one.

But wait. It actually did touch Him, and in the most broken of ways. Satan eagerly planted destruction in our hearts, intending to grow strangling vines around us to suffocate. He intended to cause our eyes to lose sight of joy, moving through the motions without really living. He wanted us to feel pain and take hit after hit from our circumstances. This very destructive brokenness, which Satan meant for eternal harm to our souls, is the very thing God uses to reach us deep inside and pull us out.

Our God is so good. He didn't bring this brokenness into the world, but instead of turning away, He became broken to be in our broken, to help us find our way back to Him even as we are broken. What the devil intended for suffering; God used for healing. He used the cracks in our hearts to breathe life into places that would otherwise be barricaded and unreachable in order to gift the fullest healing—a healing of our souls.

And, yes, that one person I'm talking about who was untouchably touched by death is Jesus. The One whom death thought it had conquered. The Who was broken apart, His very life suffocated out of Him. Did He have to go there? No. But God is love.

God sent Jesus, His Son, to earth to rescue us in the middle of our storms of brokenness. And when He came here, He brought life, hope, joy, promise and redemption. He showed us the great lengths He would go to save us; yes, to even die. And then, three days later, He showed us the even greater lengths He would go to save us. He would conquer death, which is brokenness in its very final and depleted state. Even there, He would rescue us. Brokenness, because of His grace, was made into the most powerful tool for heart transformation and for good. Brokenness flooded Jesus's soul because He wants us. He loves us. And He was willing to go there for me, for you, for my sweet Titus.

This is why. This is why sickness and death happened to my son. But this is also why I'm not afraid to go there—to broken places and to live broken.

When we hurt, the deepest need we have is for someone to be there for us. When Titus took his last breath here and ran to the arms of Jesus, we were left on this side, ripped to shreds. We called our people to come be with us. They held us and sobbed with us. They recognized the pain and let their hearts break too. They weren't afraid to be cut by the razors that had just mutilated our hearts, and they willingly stood with us and felt it all. This was love. This was the Spirit of our God with us—feeling our brokenness. In that moment, we had good brokenness. The kind that gave abundance and joy. A deep, love-filled brokenness.

Look at Jesus' scars. Reflect on the cross that was carried and died on for you and me. The scars on His body remained even after death was conquered and He was raised back to life. Why? Because He wanted you to know there is a precious gift in brokenness. The gift of His deep abiding love for you and His covenant promise to redeem.

This is the answer to my questionings of why. And it is also why I will run full-on into my broken, where I know I will indeed break free.

Ely was down for his nap. Successfully. That's an important detail. I paced the perimeter of the house. Lap completed; I began again. It was aimless. I was looking for my friends, Motivation and Inspiration. Two rounds through the house convinced me they were out and about. I would not find them here. I tried my hand at a fiction read. I made it through three short chapters before I realized there was nothing inside me to even give to this.

My mind jumped to my options. TV, Facebook, Instagram... Hmm.... Nope.

The house was quiet. Without even thinking about it, I found myself moving to the couch and curling up with Titus and Ely's favorite Boise State Snuggie®. I wasn't tired, but then again, what would I call it? I had no energy to do anything. The desire and zest for any kind of project was nonexistent.

It had been an emotional few weeks. I'm not sure the trigger, exactly. We'd passed Titus's one-year mark of going to be with Jesus. Around this time last year, we were navigating Columbus travels and the clinical trial world with Ely. I know I have lots of reasons to feel deep emotions, but I truly couldn't put my finger on what was happening in my heart and soul right in that moment. I lay down, closed my eyes. I lay still. Completely still. Which is impressive for me (ask my husband, whom I drive crazy with my constant fidgeting). My eyes opened and fell on the canvas Danny had made for me for my birthday. An incredible gift; a beautiful family picture of Danny, Ely, and I after Titus passed away, with one of my favorite pictures of Titus photoshopped in, taken just before he had turned four years old. He fit perfectly between Danny's arms and was slightly faded out, showing how close, yet how far, he was now.

I'd had more nightmares the previous night. Titus was in the end-of-life stage. In this nightmare, my son was living day after day in this last stage of life, but not leaving us. It was agony for me, as his mom, to watch him, continually questioning whether I was making the right decisions for him. I even remember crying so hard in my mother's lap as she held me, consoling me. This cry in my dream was so very similar to the soul-tearing grief that poured out of me the moment after Titus took his last breath in real life. Oh, the deep gut-wrenching decisions we had to make and hold to, knowing it was the best for Titus, even as they ripped our hearts out.

My dream transitioned and suddenly I was traveling with a young singing group. The Bekah in the dream had journeyed through a battle against Batten disease and had lost her son. She knew she was going to lose her other son as well. She just couldn't be the same Bekah that was on a similar singing tour years ago. In my dream I was so aware of how different this made me and everything felt awkward with the other tour mates. The Bekah who went through trauma was misunderstood, unfriended, alone. The only person willing to work on a dance project with her for the concert was an old man who had also lost loved ones.

Then suddenly I was in someone's house looking for medication through all their drawers. Pictures of their family showed they too either had or still had a daughter who was very sick. And another who seemed to be healthy. I knew we weren't supposed to be in their home and I wasn't sure why it was so important we find this particular medication, but suddenly I walked into a room and my son, Titus, was lying there on the edge of death. I lost it. I gathered him in my arms and sobbed. I went between praying and truly believing God was going to miraculously heal him in that very moment to knowing I would have to release him to God and say a painful goodbye. And I just couldn't.

Then I woke up. And it was all real. That last week of Titus's life on the edge of death was sweet and beautiful, yet painful and heart-killing. It slashed me apart in ways that could never come back together on this Earth.

Oh, my Titus, how I miss you and how grief on this earth, in this life, is agony.

How this has become my life, I'm not really sure. It just happened. I wonder at my evolving as a mom. And I feel a bit of a failure right now, if I'm speaking truthfully.

Ely's bedroom door creaked open at that moment and I heard a sweet "Hi" float down the hallway. I returned a sweet hello back, beckoning my son to come out to the living room. His feet pitter-pattered down the tile floor and he slid between the couch and recliner to get to where I was snuggled under the blanket. My little one, he understands the need for a good cuddle. Without hesitation, he spotted his place next to me and burrowed in. I brushed my fingers through his hair as we both quietly laid there, just being. He in his world, me in mine.

I started thinking about how I used to plan monthly themes and lessons for my boys. One month was Goodnight Moon. Titus loved that book. His first year of preschool, they had a program where they could borrow a book over the weekend from the library. His first weekend after school started, he brought home Goodnight Moon. It gave us all a good chuckle. He obviously missed the point of bringing home a new reading adventure. We read from the school copy all weekend, sent it back on Monday, and continued reading it over and over again with our copy at home in the months and years that followed. I did my mommy duty and pinned all the good stuff to teach language and comprehension from Goodnight Moon. We had a yellow chart I hung with pictures from the stories. We played matching games, made a storyboard, and practiced our words.

Ely interrupted my remembering as he hopped down from his snuggle-spot and ran over to the stuffed animal basket to grab "Snake." You might like to know we also have "Duck," "Doggie," "Neigh," and "Dumbo." But "Snake" is kinda special.

You see, I'm terrified of snakes. My brother knows this about me and has plagued me with snake images, snake videos, and even real snake skin just to watch my fears flood out of me in tears, screams, and physical fleeing. I'd like to say he's grown out of this, that he's matured now that he's in his thirties.

He hasn't.

But I have grown in tiny steps to conquer this fear. Perhaps partially to his credit (Thanks, Brad, I think). But also simply because of having boys. As I watched Ely grip Snake in his small fist, another memory worked its way through my brain.

It was Titus's second trip to the zoo. We went into the store at the end, knowing we'd likely buy something for him. I was thinking something cute and furry, but he had other ideas and went straight for the snakes hanging down the far wall of the store. I tried to detour him to the penguins, or perhaps a cute fluffy lion. But he had his eyes on a green and black snake with yellow eyes—yellow, of course, being his favorite color. After telling myself firmly that I needed to be an adult and this was truly a stuffed, fake animal that would not suddenly come to life and eat my whole family in the middle of the night, I said okay. Titus sat behind me in the car, and all the way home, he threw the snake at my head, pretending it was attacking me. Lovely. What a boy. But it made all three of us—Titus, Daddy, and me—laugh.

Back to the present, where Ely climbed back up next to me, Snake around his neck, the remaining part stretched out down next to me. Again, I wondered at my growth as a mom. In that moment I didn't feel like I was growing. I felt stale, depressed. I cuddled that snake and that cute little boy of mine in close. One tear fell out of the corner of my eye and I wondered at how it had escaped without company. Perhaps it was just enough to remind me that I could still feel. I was still here. And yeah, this life still hurt. Deeply.

So much was missing. I should be cleaning the bathrooms, I told myself. But I couldn't. I breathed; Ely breathed. I felt him, held him tight. I thought about how I used to feel Titus next to me this way. Right up to his last breath. How I missed him. My heart ached and yearned to see my two boys together again. I couldn't wait to see the two of them playing and adventuring in a pain-free, joy-filled place.

These days here feel so permanent. Hard. Like swimming through mud. And yet I keep remembering this is all so temporary. Sometimes that helps. Other times, it feels like the voice reminding me of this truth is Charlie Brown's teacher, and I can't understand a word.

There is a resolve in me, though. And knowing my current state and condition, I know it's not a resolve of mine, but of the One who is greater than all this pain and heartache. I'm held. Just as I am gifted the moment of holding Ely. I breathe. My Abba—my God Almighty who fights for me, breathes through that breath and gives me courage to take another. We repeat. I'm not conquering anything today. But I'm doing great soul work in just being.

This is hard. Breathe.

This is painful. Breathe.

I'm not alone. Big deep breath.

It's okay if all I can do is lie here next to my son. And just breathe.

Thanks for listening,

Bekah

NOTES

CHAPTER FIFTEEN

GRACE FOR EACH DAY

A nniversaries are tough.

When we first became parents, we had great anticipation for milestones worth celebrating. But then Titus's first seizure stamped a day in February, and two separate diagnoses claimed a day in April and another in June. And then, of course, that day in September was swallowed up when death finally crossed our threshold.

It felt so unfair for our annual markers to become dates symbolized by brokenness and death. Even birthdays became complicated. While we celebrated our boys growing older each year, we were acutely aware it was also a year closer to saying goodbye.

And then—*poof*—the goodbye was upon us, and then it was over, and we had nothing left but the anniversary of the hardest day of our lives.

They say the days are long, but the years are short. Boy, were they ever. With the passing of each anniversary, my heart ached for my little boy. The one who should've been starting a new school year, signing up for his first tee-ball team, measuring his ever-increasing height against his mama's.

We had lived in knowing the loss was coming, and now it was a reality.

Even when I wasn't actively thinking about my son, my subconscious was always aware of him. In the days that lead up to the anniversary of Titus's Batten Diagnosis, I felt it looming over my heart. It was the first time we'd pass this day without our son by our side. I went to sleep that night wishing I could forget the stupid day approaching, wishing it didn't have such a hold on my spirit.

As that morning approached, I was deep in sleep, dreaming that I was losing my boy all over again. While in the dream, waves of grief washed over me with the strength of an ocean roar. Gut-wrenching cries wracked my body. I couldn't hold it in. A wail, more animal than human, burst from my throat into the quiet morning hours. I tried to tell myself I was dreaming in an attempt to wake myself up, but grief had imprisoned me, and there was no escape from it. Danny leaned over me. He called my name over and over. I felt his arms come around me, holding me, telling me it was okay.

And that's how we began another year of the anniversary of Titus's diagnosis.

The thing with memorable days, good or bad, is that we *remember*.

I remember the anxiety I felt the night before, all those years ago, knowing we'd be marching into the doctor's office the next morning to hear the results they had discovered.

And I remember the shock, grief, and loss that crushed us when we heard the word "Batten" for the first time on April 7, 2015, at 11:45 AM.

Those moments will never leave me.

Before Batten disease, my years started fresh at the same time everyone else's did: January 1. Then the first diagnosis came, and April 7 became my new year marker. And then September 17 replaced it as we ushered Titus into eternity. All year, every year, I look back each day and remember: *A year ago today, Titus or Ely (fill in the blank).*

So many milestones gained and then lost. How have I survived?

One night, I was standing in the kitchen cleaning up dinner. From the living room, I heard Danny playing a video of Titus. His little voice and dinosaur roar pierced my soul. I smiled on the outside, choosing to remember with fondness. On the inside, my soul was bleeding through the pierced hole, crying with pain. What a gift, this video, but what agony. I wondered: Will I always have to feel the agony?

How have I survived? And more, how have I thrived?

Is it because I've turned into a superhero, able to rise above all emotions and circumstances, plowing through each day? I think we all know the answer... No.

Is it because I was made for this sort of thing? This story, these circumstances, that so many others say they would never survive? Is it because I just naturally fit the role? No.

Is it because I must be in denial and stuffing away my feelings and emotions, refusing to face the truth? You guessed it: No.

I can explain my survival through one word.

GRACE.

Period.

That my superior God looked down at inferior me and chose me—gave FAVOR to me!

That He allowed my heart to open, not close. My eyes to see, not burn. Love experienced, not shut out.

That He gifted me laughter, perspective, joy—not bitterness.

That He held me in the dark rather than hiding from me.

That He allowed me to see gifts all around me.

In the twinkle of my son's eye—there it was! A gift!

In the giggle that began deep in the throat and exploded out, face lifted to the sky (because that's the proper way to laugh with abandon)—there it was! A gift!

In the warm hug that held me even after I'd spoken bitter words, tried to drive it away. There it was. A gift.

In the teachers, nurses, and therapists who embraced my boys with love and one-of-a-kind care, giving it all they had. A gift!

In the support, love, and events that brought us together with our village, showing we weren't doing this life alone. The stories of people changed, loving BIG, and God working through the boys and through others' generosity. A gift!

In the calming, centered peace of my kitchen counter as I sipped on a cup of tea and talked to my God. Oh, what a gift.

In the encouraging words on cards, scrawled out beautifully, giving us glimpses of authentic love. A gift.

In the community of love and pledged journeying together—a commitment to do life with us no matter the cost. A gift!

The way I could fall apart mentally and still rise a different kind of brave. A gift.

It is all a gift of GRACE!

In no way did I, Bekah, do anything majestic or astonishing or particularly breathtaking to deserve acts of such unbelievable grace.

Who does that? Who extends grace like that? We selfish and limited mortals—do we, on our own, create that kind of power of freedom and love?

Simply stated?

We could never.

Not on our own.

What we have the holy honor of being, are conveyors of God's grace. God's grace centers me, grounds me. I don't want to miss it, this gift of grace.

I could fool myself into believing the reason I have His favor is because of how much good I do. That I've earned it. But let me tell you, I can't even begin to live under that pressure. There is no number of good deeds I could have done to earn what my God has given me in love, grace, mercy, wisdom, and perspective. I could not make enough good choices, be kind or giving enough to change the situation. I cannot redeem this disease, this brokenness. I can't. I CAN'T.

But my God can. My God lives in an economy of grace. He works in an economy that looks like this: *You owe, Bekah. It's your heartbreak, Bekah. It's your problem, Bekah. But I'll pay. I'll redeem. I'll hold you. I'll stand beside you in the raging current. I'll listen to you, whether you praise my name or curse at me. I'll be there to celebrate with you. I'll be there to mourn with you. I'll pay, Bekah. I'll pay.*

This deeply rooted need I have for my Abba Father is not a back-burner priority. It isn't a box I check off the list once I've attended church or read my Bible. It isn't an extracurricular activity that I add to my life as I feel like it.

It's everything.

He is my source of life. His grace is what gives me the ability to smile. It's what keeps me in check when I say something against my fellow human. It's what causes me to feel, deeply. It's what gives me strength to keep getting up each day. It's what gives me the ability to choose bravery and courage no matter what is dealt to me. It's what brings me back to love, thankfulness, joy.

This gift of grace is for me—and it's for you. As I cling to hope and redemption of all this pain, I pray you also feel the love of a good, good Father who loves you.

NOTES

CHAPTER SIXTEEN

IT'S ALL
IN THE ROOTS

I must take you back to October 2015, just 6 months after our diagnosis. Titus's health was failing fast. After getting Titus off to school, I sat down at the kitchen bar, my journal in hand.

I could not comprehend how we were surviving. And not just surviving, but thriving! I felt joy, peace and hope. My perspective had shifted, the blinders had come off, and I could see redemption happening in the present.

I could see a good God at work in our story and weaving ours through others as we all joined in His Big Story–the greatest story ever told.

I claimed truth and put lies to rest. And as a result, fear and anxiety were laid to rest too.

I found power in gratitude and in slowing down to live each moment intentionally.

None of this made sense to my weak, limited ability to change our situation.

I think of Abraham and the covenant promise God made with him. This became Abraham's anticipated gift as he journeyed through a life that didn't quite make sense according to what God had promised.

For one, God had promised Abraham many, many descendants. There was one blaring problem. He was childless. But this promise ignited in Abraham a focus for his life decisions and became a beacon of truth-light to follow. He practiced obedience to God, and repentance when that obedience didn't go so well. He experienced God's blessings, God's correction, and yes—God's faithfulness. We see today that God indeed held up His end of the covenant to Abraham.[5]

As I sat there in my reflection, pen in hand, I began to write. What poured out of me was a promise, a manifesto, if you will.

CAN'T STEAL MY JOY MANIFESTO

Wanna know why I can't be plucked from the garden of joy? When that hand of hate, jealousy, anger, bitterness, or selfishness tries to pull me out, my roots cling tight, dive deep, wrap around the other roots that are growing deep. So when the evil one tries to pull my flower out, he really has to contend with a mass of roots that have intertwined below.

This web of deep, strong roots is a result of God's love. He is deep in us. When we face a storm on the surface—my leaves and petals taking a beating no flower could appear to endure—He holds tight to my roots and weaves them through the roots of other flowers so that it isn't just me that's hanging on to truth. It's me plus a whole system of support.

It's because of that support that, as the storm goes on, I don't wilt. I don't become uprooted. I firmly stand my ground in the soil of LIFE. And others around me do too! God has woven us together and we will stand strong, united and beautiful in the storm.

We will add radiant colors in the gray skies, sweet smells as bitter rain comes down because our roots are

d

e

e

p.

It doesn't matter what happens on the surface–deep is where our roots are pulling nutrients. HE is providing everything we need to stay up.

But... we do look beaten.

Save us, Lord! You see our plight and you cling tight. I might feel this unimaginable storm, but you keep together the most important part of me–my soul.

When I, a summer flower, bloom in the dead of frigid winter, people wonder, How?

My roots.

My roots are held deep in love and warmth, surviving and thriving in unthinkable conditions. You give life that doesn't make sense, Lord. It appears impossible to live in such a way, a bloomed flower in the dead of winter. Only a good, redemptive God can give that kind of life. Thank you for deep roots in you. For clinging to me deep in my soul so I can survive. Thank you for winding my roots around the strong, wise roots of others.

You have won and will continue to win in my heart.

Nothing can hold you back. So please, Lord, radiate strong from my being, through my broken stem and beaten leaves, right to my new and beautiful bloom. My broken stem shows my weakness, and my new bloom shows that You take brokenness and make it SO beautiful.

Thank you, Lord. Oh, how I love You. Bloom beautiful in me, despite my ugly, broken stem.

I read over the fresh writing passionately scribbled across the page. It dawned on me that God had just gifted me a very special promise. A covenant. A beacon of truth-light to guide my difficult days. I tucked it away as a treasure, holding on to the promise of a blooming flower hanging by a thread off a broken stem, deeply rooted in love, hope and redemption; expressing joy that didn't make sense. This broken, blooming flower was my life.

Time moved ever so quickly. As I held on to the clear vision God had given me of a broken, blooming flower rooted deep in His love and redemption, I found life in it. I knew we were blooming when it didn't make sense, and I felt a sense of joy and thankfulness for those short days with Titus. We dived deep into learning to love big and live intentionally in each and every moment. We built and nurtured relationships because that was most important to us. After all, our community equaled our roots. I'm not all that good at math, but that equation came out right every time.

A short 11 months after this manifesto promise was gifted to me, we said goodbye for now to Titus and we jumped into the clinical trial world with Ely.

In November 2016, an entire year since God had gifted me such a special promise, Ely came home with a pot of dirt from church. Of course, it spilled on the way home in the car. (I mean, why wouldn't a big open pot of dirt sit nicely on the ride home?) I had the worst attitude about it, huffing and whining as I scooped the dirt up, throwing it into the pot. Danny, our plant whisperer, told me to set it out on the patio to see if anything would grow. I set it out there, dusted my hands off, and moved on.

Nothing happened those first couple weeks. It appeared Danny was watering dirt. Just dirt. Then, one day, this tiny little green bud popped out. Danny was so proud (he really can make anything grow). We watched our little plant grow and grow until it opened up into this gorgeous flower.

Its color?

Yellow.

What a sweet treasure, as we thought of our yellow-loving boy every time we looked at it. It bloomed proud and perfect.

Until... (Doesn't brokenness have a way of finding us everywhere?)

One day Danny was out chopping wood for an upcoming camping trip. A splinter flew off to one side and chopped that bloom right off. We were so sad. We really grieved our poor flower's sudden death. The beauty on our patio diminished on that day in a real, tangible way. But time moved on, as it always does, unaffected by our grief or circumstances.

The following Sunday, my sister and I were having conversation over coffee. Danny and Michael, my brother-in-law, were out on the patio working on projects.

Knock, knock, knock.

The guys were trying to get our attention. I rounded the corner and saw Michael waving us over, a flower pot clutched in his hands. I was confused at first, but as I got closer and caught sight of what he held, I felt God wrap me up in a giant bear hug as He whispered, "You are still beautiful in this broken grief because you are my child—held in beloved victory."

In Michael's hand was that poor flower who had met the death of splintered wood the week before, but it looked different. This flower had a stem broken almost completely off; holes chewed and torn through the leaves. Life had broken it down. But the most miraculous thing was happening on the end of that damaged, dangling stem.

The flower was blooming bright, full and yellow, singing to the world of its glory... no, rather of God's glory. And that glory-proclaiming was deeply rooted in the system of that flower in the pot. Its roots were woven deep and intertwined, holding it down in a place of nourishment and stability amidst chaos. The bloom screamed hope in the shadow of death and redemption right here, right now. There was beauty happening in the midst of the ugly, and this bloom captivated us with its impossible strength and stunning beauty.

This flower before me was the very same promise God had given me for the life we were journeying. Hanging at an angle just like the flower I wrote about in my journal back in October 2015, was this incredible yellow bloom. It spoke through its beauty to my heart, saying, *"Nothing can steal my joy."*

I was in awe at this gift. For God to have reached down in such a way to plant such deep symbolism in my mind in 2015 and then actually create such a scene on my back patio in 2016... Wow!

I thought of all we'd journeyed through in that time. A brand-new, heartbreaking diagnosis for both of our boys. The steep learning curve of advocacy. The fight to give my child freedom as Batten Disease stripped it away. The firm grasp we held to living in the moment and adventuring as a family, no matter the conditions.

And then the "lasts" with Titus. The last time we'd celebrate Halloween, Thanksgiving, Christmas, Easter, his birthday with him. The last time we'd hear him laugh or see him smile. The last time we'd take him to school. The last time we'd watch him take a breath; a breath that was his last here on Earth, but also served as a launching pad to Jesus.

And then our firsts. Our first chance at fighting against this disease and taking Ely to Ohio for surgery and infusions. All this and so much more took place between these two events—my vision in 2015 and God's creative outpouring of glory on my back patio in 2016.

Through all this time, I became so very aware of two things.

My brokenness.

His redemption.

And really, aren't we all broken? You know what your broken stem and beaten leaves are. We all have them. But at the end of that broken stem is a redemptive bloom. One that reflects the unchanging beauty of Christ that is in ALL of us.

When our eyes become unblinded and we can truly see our beautiful redemptive blooms, our gaze is set on truth. We look up to Him, not down and around at our circumstances. Our hope is not based on life storms that come at us, but in a consistent, promise-keeping God.

Perhaps, when our focus is on that glory-filled bloom, our stems and leaves become (dare I say it?) inconsequential?

Not because they don't hurt anymore... oh, they do! But because we can see beyond the hurt and know that hope is always worth holding on to. Redemption is coming–and in fact, is already happening here and now. Our God is victorious!

As I felt the faith community surround us, I pictured our roots all held together. As I smiled authentically in a moment where perhaps fearful tears would've made more sense, I pictured my bloom. When I would cry, curled in a ball on the floor, unable to do one more thing that day, I pictured my broken stem and beaten leaves. And then I'd remember my roots. And I'd get up and keep going.

Oh friend, may you see your bloom. May you know deep in your soul just how much Jesus loves you. I mean, really, really loves you.

Hold on. Hold on to those hope-filled roots, God's strength and victory always before you, beside you, under you, and all around you.

"I pray that from his glorious, unlimited resources he will empower you with inner strength through his Spirit. Then Christ will make his home in your hearts as you trust in him. Your roots will grow down into God's love and keep you strong. And may you have the power to understand, as all God's people should, how wide, how long, how high and how deep his love is. May you experience the love of Christ, though it is too great to understand fully. Then you will be made complete with all the fullness of life and power that comes from God. Now all glory to God, who is able, through his mighty power at work within us, to accomplish infinitely more than we might ask or think. Glory to him in the church and in Christ Jesus through all generations forever and ever. Amen."
Ephesians 3:16-21 (NLT)

NOTES

EPILOGUE

WHERE ARE WE NOW?

We are mere weeks away from this book releasing and as I type one-handed, my other arm holds a sleeping six-year-old love bug in my lap. Ely is currently getting his 77th brain infusion; the clear, unassuming fluid dripping into his port to be delivered to his central nervous system where all the little enzymes will go to work cleaning up his cells. This is what keeps him alive, peacefully napping in my arms. Truth be told, we don't know what the future holds. There is no way to predict how long these synthetic enzymes can keep deterioration at bay, but they are doing a remarkable job at slowing this Batten monster down. In the meantime, I am going to keep looking up at God's upper story. I'm going to pause so I can remember and celebrate. I'm going to live in this moment right now, knowing I get to witness redemption and victory even here in the mundane and broken. These are lessons I keep re-learning and gifts God keeps revealing.

Because life seems to change often (and sometimes rapidly), I invite you to head over to *www.cantstealmyjoy.com/where-are-we-now* for a full update.

See you there, friend.

ACKNOWLEDGMENTS

F riends, there are so many people to thank. I fear I am going to forget someone! The reality is, it's impossible to name every person who has made this book possible. I don't even personally know all the names. Throughout our journey, thousands of friends and strangers made their generosity accessible to us, whether it was through donations, beautiful cards and gifts, sharing our story, and praying for us. We call you our Team—Team 4 Titus and Ely (thank you Carrie for starting our page way back in the beginning). We met you on social media, on one of our many airplane rides, at church, events, conferences, in our neighborhoods, and through the magical interconnectedness of God's big story. I have loved watching Him weave His goodness and love all throughout our little journeys. What we do to support one another might feel small, but it is all so eternal.

When we moved back to Idaho in the fall of 2018, it was an unexpected change. While it was incredibly difficult leaving our support system, jobs, and friends in California, it was a blessing to move back "home" closer to Titus and Ely's Grandparents. In the transition, my mother-in-law offered her home to us while we looked for a house of our own. During the 9 months she and her husband generously opened her home and space to us, I wrote this book. Because we didn't have a house payment to worry about at that time, I was able to put off job-searching and buckle down to write. To Eddie and Cindy—thank you for supporting us during the transition and making space for this dream of mine to come true. Love you both!

I still remember sitting across from Anne Riley at the Batten conference, the summer of 2017. She had written a beautiful children's book that, still to this day, I cannot talk about without crying. (Seriously, go get Voyage to the Star Kingdom on Amazon—it's one of the most beautifully written books about life storms, death, and eternal life and is based on the story of some very dear friends of ours.) I felt such a connection with Anne and emailed her later to share that I had stories in my heart too, but I didn't know how to get them out. Anne became a cheerleader and an accountability to me. She also did the first round of edits on this book and helped me find and keep my unique voice while clarifying the message of what I wanted to say. Anne heard all my weird worries, fears and excitement as I journeyed the book writing process for the first time. Her voice kept me going and her expertise gave me the next right steps I needed to plug away. I am convinced I would have given up long ago if she hadn't helped me celebrate each step and encouraged me to keep going. Anne, thank you for being a safe place for me to test out this writing thing and the many emotions that go with it. You are a gift!

Jessica Salas—the ever so talented cover designer of this book, ladies and gentlemen! Jess and I go back, before I ever knew of her amazing graphic design talents, to our days at MOPS. It was there I met an infectiously joyful leader who spread the love of Jesus through her smile, her actions, and her spirit. When I found out she did graphic design, I emailed her an idea I had for the cover of this book. As she read my words and created those words into a picture, she was on point. The vision in my head felt out of reach, but when she got a hold of the vision, it became a beautiful reality. Jess, you have been a delight to partner with on this project and your friendship is truly a blessing. Thank you!

Anna—when we sat across from each other, barely acquaintances at the time, and I shared about the vision of the flower with you, I never dreamed of the friendship that would become rooted there and bloom. You took the artwork God created on our patio and gave it a digital blueprint, creating a way for me to share with the world the message of hope, love and redemption. Thank you for saying yes. For jumping on board with my crazy ideas and for seeing beauty in the broken. Love you, friend.

To my beta reading team: Jody, Kelly and Dawna—You three hit it out of the park. Thank you for your honest feedback, both affirming and "hey, this is confusing and needs to be different" types of feedback. It was nerve-wracking sharing this piece of work, but each of you held it with such grace and care. For that, I thank you. Your partnership in this, made all the clearer, what God had for me to say, and your encouragement propelled me forward to keep saying it. For all your time, critique, and affirmations, thank you!

Sara, your willingness to take the time from your busy schedule as pastor, wife, and mom to be my final proofreader meant the world to me. Thank you for taking a weight off my shoulders and agreeing to read it for a final pass-through on fresh eyes. Your friendship will always be special to me. I will forever remember Titus and Ava holding hands running around the park just before we departed Illinois for our California move. Those are sweet memories I cherish, friend. So glad to do life with you.

To my hope*writer friends—oh, how God knew I would need you all in order to see this project through. Once I completed the manuscript, life got busy. Ely's needs increased, we moved into a new home, and I started a brand-new job in a field I had never worked in before. You kept me anchored in the writing world, reminding me why we write, and keeping me accountable and encouraged, not just through checking in with me, but through sharing your own journeys of writing in the midst of life. You are incredible followers of Jesus, declaring light in the spaces God has called you to, and I am honored to be a witness to your journeys.

As I got near the end of my editing and it came time to begin formatting and designing the interior of the book, I started having panic attacks, migraines, and nightmares over doing this part of the book correctly, knowing it was a learning curve I didn't have room for on my timeline. To Taryn, of Typewriter Creative Co., you took a burden off me and allowed me to enjoy this part of the book making process. Thank you for your expertise, your timeliness, and your incredible talents. I felt I was being a good steward of this story bringing you on board, because you would make the reader experience so much more beautiful. Thank you!

And to all of you (you know who you are) who persistently encouraged me to write a book, thank you. You called out a gift in me and I count myself blessed to have so many individuals in my life who care enough to do so. And to those who believed so much in it, you talked about it on your platforms, shared on your podcasts and blogs, and advertised in your magazines—thank you!

To my parents, James and Carolyn, thank you for raising me in a home where we loved Jesus and each other in really big ways. The foundation you laid out for me prepared me for the storms ahead. Thank you for always empowering me in my passions and holding me in my failures. You taught me that I was loved and beloved by my God, no matter what I succeeded in or screwed up. Thank you for your wisdom, your example, and your love. (Mama bear hugs and butterfly kisses!)

To my hubs, Danny—Hun, you have been my biggest critique and my loudest cheerleader (even if the two got a bit confusing at times...). All along the way, you pushed me to break through my walls of fear and called things out of me I didn't always recognize for myself. Your support and encouragement took me from closet-writing status to actually calling myself a writer. It still feels a little weird to claim that title, but I am proud of it and I couldn't have done it without you. Thank you for sacrificing many nights of quality time together so I could write and edit (and edit, and edit, and edit). Thank you for investing in this story, both in real life and on paper—believing along with me that it needed to make its way into the world. You are the only other person who understands what it is like, as a parent, to lose our son and fight for our other. We are bound together always as we journey hard places and find joy and goodness. I love you.

NOTES

BLOG ENTRY: MAY 2015

1. Ann Voskamp, One Thousand Gifts, (Grand Rapids: Zondervan, 2010), 33

BLOG ENTRY: AUGUST 2015

2. Ann Voskamp, One Thousand Gifts, (Grand Rapids: Zondervan, 2010), 97

CHAPTER 9: EXPECTANT ANTICIPATION

3. Story of Joseph, Genesis 37-50

BLOG ENTRY: FEBRUARY 2016

4. Story of The Temptation of Jesus, Matthew 4:1-17

CHAPTER 16: IT'S ALL IN THE ROOTS

5. Story of Abraham, Genesis 12-25

ABOUT THE AUTHOR

Bekah was born and raised in Idaho. She, her husband and boys have had the privilege of living in the Midwest, Southern California and Idaho—twice! She loves every place they've called home because of the people they did life with along the way.

Bekah graduated with a degree in psychology and a minor in children's ministry and launched into ministry after graduation. She served as a children's pastor in Idaho, Illinois, and California and assumed it would be a lifelong career. But then Batten came beating on their door. She stepped out of the workforce to be home full-time. Those years at home were precious. It was during that time; she discovered a love for writing that would move beyond her journal entries. Bekah shares her work across different publications now and enjoys being part of God's redemptive and hope-filled story in this way.

Besides writing, Bekah is passionate about bridging the gap between churches and families with disabilities. Because she was a children's pastor for several years and then a rare disease mama, she identifies with both sides of the struggle. Her hope is to use her knowledge and experience to help church become a place of belonging for everyone.

When she isn't writing, you might find Bekah at the office working as the Volunteer Manager for her community's local Guardian ad Litem (CASA) program, spending time with her hubby and son and two dogs, or jumping in on an indoor soccer game. She loves coffee, fresh journals, and meaningful conversation. And most of all, she loves being a small part of God's Big Story.

CONNECT
WITH BEKAH

Facebook @Team4TitusEly
Instagram @cantstealmyjoy2
Web www.cantstealmyjoy.com
Email bekah@cantstealmyjoy.com

Today you and I get to be part of the greatest story ever told.
Here's to journeying together.

69023914R00113

Made in the USA
Middletown, DE
18 September 2019